YOU CAN'T WIN
IF YOU DON'T ENTER

Carolyn Wilman

ISBN 10: 1-4196-8969-X
ISBN 13: 978-1-4196-8969-7
Library of Congress Control Number: 2008901262
To order additional copies, contact:
Imagination Edge Inc.
www.contestqueen.com
1.866.231.6676
orders@contestqueen.com

DEDICATION

For all those who helped me make my dreams come true:
Mom, Dad, Laura, Ryan, Len, Piri and especially Craig and Nicole.
Thank you for helping me to become a *winner*!

In memoriam:
Lynn Marie Banks Goutbeck
co-author of Winning Ways
March 10, 1952—April 28, 2005

ACKNOWLEDGEMENTS

I am truly grateful for all those that helped me write this book and make it a success.

Amanda Adams, Charmaine B., Victoria Barber, Paul Beuger, Janice Bodinet, Scott Bourgeois, Harriet Brown, Terry Brown, Amy Canganelli, Bill Carey, Ken and Diane Carlos, Carol Colvin, Jennifer Day, ShariAnne Fischer, John Findlay, Shelly G., Joyce Gilliam, Sandra Grauschopf, Parry Grubb, Sandy Gulliver, Bob Gunther, Linda Horricks, Chuck Humphrey, Cindy Kuptz, Lisa LaFreniere, Lisa Lantz, Vincent Lavoie, Andrew Lustigman, Billy and Angela Mabray, Craig McDaniel, Ron Miller, Dana Noga, Patti Osterheld, Vince Pelss, Brent Riley, Melanie Rockett, Shelly Rowan, Allen and Carolyn Sayward, John Sayward, Shannon Shoemaker, Carl Slawinski, Jay Sloofman, Adam Solomon, Ingrid Stamatson, Nick Taylor, Bernard Tiraloche, Phil Van Treuren, Karen Weix, Al Wester.

To all the sweepstakes club members because they taught me that friendship is the best prize of this hobby: Paula A., Sharon A., Vicki A., Patricia B., Alice Bruns, Karen C., Patty C., Marge D., Steve D., Valerie D., Nadine F., Ret F., Steve F., Tom F., Judy G., Rebecca G., Deb H., Jo-Anne H., Kim H., Linda H., Ingrid J., Mike and Julie J., Mary K., Nancy K., Maureen Kennerk, Angela M., Arlene M., Brenda M., Judy M., Kathy M., Nancy M., Maria Miller, Ann N., Patricia N., Linda P., Amy S., Cindy S., Diane S., Laura S., Rita S., Sharon S., Dortha Schaefer, Joyce T., Gail W., Betty Yearling.

To all those that regaled me with wonderful, and often funny, stories of their sweepstaking adventures: Aimee-Baldwinsville NY, Al-Dearborn MI, Bea-Toronto ON, Carmen-Norfolk VA, Evelyn-Queen Anne MD, Joe-Colona IL, Mary-St. Albert AB, Polli-Rockville MD, Rachel-Morrisville NC, Susan-Rose Bay NS, Terry-Fairport NY, Tina-Wapakoneta OH, Tracy-Burke VA, Vickie-Dallas OR.

Carol McLaughlin, who converted me from a contestor into a sweeper.

Bob Mennell, who answered my seemingly endless list of tax-related questions.

Richard Adams, Kevin Amery, and Stephanie Serba who patiently edited and reedited this book.

Mark Lobo (www.dozegfx.com) who designed a polished book cover and a very striking user-friendly website.

I want to give an extra special thank you to Scott Cruickshank who during our interview stated, "You can't win if you don't enter." and I knew it was to be the name of this book.

And finally, Craig Borysowich, my husband, who wrote the chapter Spyware, Viruses and Spam OH MY! Thank you for providing all the information technology know-how to make this book complete.

TABLE OF CONTENTS

FOREWORD

I love getting packages in the mail, and I always have. I grew up on a farm in Minnesota, and weeks could go by without seeing another human being outside of our family. The mailman was our link to the outside world. The best part of any day was to look out the window and see a brown paper package (yes…tied up with string) hanging from the mailbox. There were nine of us kids, and we all would race out to the box at the end of our driveway, hoping the contents of the package would be for us. It could have been anything; a trinket ordered from the back of a cereal box to clothing ordered from Sears. Whatever it was, our day was brighter for it.

50 years have passed, and a package stuffed inside the mailbox still brings the same thrill. Now, just as then, I do what I can to generate a continual stream of mail, and a padded envelope causes just as much excitement as a flat FedEx envelope containing an affidavit for a larger prize.

I entered my first sweepstakes at age 14 while leafing through a copy of one of my teen magazines. They were giving away a trip to have a date with Bobby Vinton. In 1962, he was quite the heartthrob, and I was sure I would win that date. I did not win it, but my desire for entering sweepstakes was not entirely squelched as a result of that early loss. I may have put entering sweepstakes on the back burner for several years, but the desire never stayed buried, and once adulthood settled in, I started entering everything I could get my hands on. I thought I was the only one with such steadfastness until a sample copy of Contest Newsletter came in the mail. Their readers were winning the very same sweeps I was entering, so while I knew I had company in my hobby, I also knew "someone really does win those things." There was no stopping me after that, and I set my mind to winning with even more passion. And win I did, with a string of four cars, 40 plus trips, TV's of every size and shape, and several large cash prizes of $10,000 and more.

I believe my success is a result of not relying too much on luck. I did not leave a stone unturned in my research on how drawings were conducted; the different methods of entering (and the benefits of one over the other); and just keeping abreast of the many changes in playing the different "games of chance" over the years. Whereas when I started seriously entering sweepstakes 25 years ago, my hobby is nothing like it was back then. I was successful then, and by keeping up with the changes, I am successful now.

Some of my own readers at SweepSheet® do not want to "keep up" with the changes, and their win lists show it. The bottom line is, you get out of the hobby what you put into it. So, yes, continue to enter any sweepstakes you can where they still allow you to enter by mail, but take seriously the changes such as entering online, via text messaging, and getting game codes off of product packages to send back for second chance drawings. If you do, your mailboxes, just like mine, will continue to be stuffed with 'brown paper packages'. As for me? I am trying to win a trip to Branson, MO to see Bobby Vinton.

Sandy Gulliver
Former Editor, SweepSheet®
www.sweepsheet.com

"Everything in life is luck."
Donald Trump

INTRODUCTION

I *love* entering sweepstakes. I get such a thrill out of finding new ones and reading about all the different prizes that I could win, I get butterflies in my stomach. I daydream about all the various trips I could take, the cars I could drive, or what I would spend the cash on. I *love* getting notified I won a prize. I get all bubbly inside and I grin from ear to ear for hours. ***I am passionate about sweeping.***

HOW WINNING CHANGED MY LIFE

I have good reason to feel this way. Sweeping has actually changed the course of my life. Winning prizes back in 1991 lead to going on a trip to Barbados with my mom… and to the first date I had with my husband.

It was early December 1990 and a popular Toronto radio station was broadcasting their morning show for a week in a large downtown department store's window. I worked in a nearby office tower and every day I would stop to watch and listen. One morning, they gave away prize packs including tickets to the Ice Capades and a gift certificate for a trendy hair salon, to the first person that could show them a photo of children in their family. I whipped open my wallet and flashed the photo of my little cousins, winning the prize pack.

My mom had been home with the flu, so when I got home I gave her the gift certificate to the hair salon. (All you ladies will understand; I had been having my hair cut by the same hairstylist for five years— almost twenty now—and would never get my hair done anywhere else *even if I won it*!) We decided that when she felt better we would spend the day together; going to the salon, having lunch and Christmas shopping downtown.

The restaurant we had lunch at that day was giving away a trip to Barbados. As we left the restaurant, I realized I forgot to get the sweepstakes entry forms. I made Mom wait as I ran back inside. When I returned I told her I would fill the forms out later, since the restaurant was close to my office. I said, "If I win I'll take you and if you win you'll take me!"

On December 24th, we were all at home wrapping gifts in the living room when the phone rang. Mom went into the kitchen to answer the call. I could only hear her side of the conversation. The woman identified herself and stated my mom may have won a trip. Mom really doesn't like telemarketers and couldn't figure out what was going on, but since it was Christmas she decided not to hang up right away. The woman asked my mom, "Where is Barbados?" My Mom nearly said she didn't know. Instead, she said, "In the Caribbean." She was told she did in fact win the trip and the travel agency would contact her in January to make all the arrangements. My Mom was confused and asked, "How did I win this trip?" I heard that and screamed, "We won! We won!" The woman asked her, "Didn't you fill out a sweepstakes entry form?" My mom said, "I think one of my kids entered me," as I jumped up and down around her.

NOTE: In Canada, we are notified we are a "potential" winner and must correctly answer a Skill Testing Question before we are declared the "official" winner. (See chapter, You're a Winner!)

TIP: Remember to tell your friends and family when you have entered them in sweepstakes. This way they won't be caught off guard when they are contacted and inadvertently disqualify themselves.

We went the following April. It was really special to spend a whole week alone with my mom—we had the best time and we learned a lot about each other.

I always wanted to win another family trip so that my mom, my daughter and I could go together. November 2005 we won a trip for four to London, England. It was so much fun to go on another vacation with not only my mom, and daughter, but my husband as well!

TIP: If you wish to take children on the trip, read the rules and check out the destination's website to ensure children are allowed at the resort or hotel. It would be a shame to win a vacation for the family, only to discover that only you and your partner can go.

So that's how I won the trip to Barbados, but I know some of you are wondering about that first date with my husband. Well, remember the four tickets to the Ice Capades I said I won? I gave away one set to a girlfriend in my office. Then I started inviting friends to see who would like to go with me. I must have invited thirty people—no one wanted to go. One day I was speaking to Craig, who at the time was a business acquaintance, and asked him to go with me. Unlike those thirty other people, *he* said yes. We had a great time. *I* thought I had made a new friend; *he* says it was our first date and I just didn't know it. We just celebrated our 12th wedding anniversary. Would we have begun a true friendship had I not won those tickets? Who knows?

My Best Win—EVER!

I continued to enter sweepstakes sporadically until I read an article that led me to become a "sweeper." (*For complete definitions see the NOTE later in this chapter.*) At the time, I had been unemployed for the longest period I have ever experienced in my professional life. One night I was lying in bed, reading the August 2001 copy of Reader's Digest, when I came across an article called "Get in the Winner's Circle! Tips from a contest junkie who's proven that the best things in life *are* free" by Barb Taylor. I read and reread that article and as I did, I made a decision—from then on, I would *win* all the things I wanted in life; like a new car!

Get in the Winner's Circle!

Tips from a contest junkie who's proven that the best things in life *are* free

by Barb Taylor, from Calgary Herald

Vacations in Italy, Hawaii and Mexico. Doing rolls in a stunt plane or being whisked off in a limousine for a night of wining, dining and theatre. Hardly the lifestyle you'd expect for an average-income family of four living in a duplex and driving a rusty old Volvo. Certainly not the lifestyle we envisioned when I left my teaching job 12 years ago to become a stay-at-home mom.

Our magical life began in 1988 after a sleepless night spent attending to our newborn son. The following day I entered a contest sponsored by a local radio station, inviting listeners to send letters to Santa. I pleaded with Santa for one night of uninterrupted sleep. My entry was selected for a one-week trip to Lake Tahoe from radio station CJAY 92. I was hooked.

Now I enter lots of contests, anywhere from 200 to 300 a year. I find out about them while shopping for groceries, listening to the radio, browsing through magazines and regularly perusing a contest newsletter to which I subscribe. Over the years, I've spent three to four hours a week researching new contests and filling out forms.

But the hard work has paid off. I averaged $10,000 in annual winnings; I've won two Dirt Devils through the Safeway Score & Win; and I've gone on a total of 14 major trips thanks to this winning hobby. My writing talents have won me a fair share of prizes as well, everything from a pair of $1,000 earrings for a local magazine's limerick contest to a pair of lift tickets for a Calgary Herald-sponsored Ski Memories contest.

Our winnings have also included clothing, appliances, a backyard barbecue and a patio set. We rarely pay to go to a movie or theatrical production. We frequently dine on gift certificates we have won. The luxuries our income doesn't provide for, my contesting does. Even our children get in on the act and have won a bike, a skateboard and passes to local attractions.

We've watched beautiful sunsets in Maui (courtesy of the Lite 96 jet) and Oahu (thanks to KissFM), walked the Freedom Trail in Boston (Calgary Co-op supermarket and Kraft foods), and even sent my in-laws to Scotland (a cross-Canada random draw from United Distillers). Will it ever end? Not as long as I can fill out an entry for or clip a Universal Product Code, or UPC as it's known (the bar code on products you buy).

Most of the trips I have won fall into the middle "good-and besides it's free" category. While not all-inclusive, your major costs of airfare and accommodation are covered. You stay in above average accommodation, usually a three-star hotel. You are generally responsible for your own meals, spending money and, occasionally, airport taxes. Trips we've won in this category included a one-week trip to San José del Cabo at the tip of Mexico's Baja peninsula. We enjoyed beautiful, uncrowded beaches, drinkable water, and simple but clean accommodations.

My husband and I experienced our "dream come true" trip courtesy of a local real-estate developer. By dropping off three entry forms at a tour of show homes, we won a one-week trip to Florence, which included stopovers in Paris and London. In Florence, we stayed at the Hotel Brunelleschi in a $650-a-night room that had floor-to-ceiling louvered windows opening onto a tiny flowered courtyard. We had a breathtaking view of the Duomo and the Campanile.

Nowadays, friends often rub my arm for luck before they head off to buy their lottery tickets. I can only shake my head in wonder—I've never won anything in a lottery.

So, you must be wondering, how do I do it? In the world of contesting, luck really has nothing to do with it: it all comes down to effort and persistence. For every contest I win, there are a 100 I've lost. Here are some suggestions to put the odds in your favor:

DO

☑ Pick free contests. These are usually drawbox contests and can be found in grocery stores and other businesses. Radio and television phone-in contests also cost nothing to enter.

☑ Also, pick the "better odds" contest: Look for contests that have a limited contesting area, offer lots of prizes, require you to "do something" (write a story, solve a puzzle), or that run for a short time span.

☑ Enter often. If it's a "better odds" contest, I'll enter five to 20 times. Try to space your entry mailings throughout the length of the contest's running.

☑ Collect UPCs. Remember that hand-drawn facsimiles are usually accepted in mail-in contests, and believe me, they really work. I've won many contests using hand-drawn facsimiles.

☑ Subscribe to a newsletter detailing currently running contests. A good one is the Canadian Contest Newsletter, P.O. Box 776, Stn. U, Etobicoke, Ont. M8Z 5P9. On the web, you can find them at: www.canadian.contests.com.

DON'T

☒ Don't swipe the entry pads and then stuff the draw box. Getting greedy may get you disqualified for taking unfair advantage.

8

☒ Don't try to win more than once a month on a given radio station. If you make a nuisance of yourself by trying to win every prize offered, you lower your chances of winning something you really want.

☒ Don't waste money sending in dozens, or hundreds, of entries to a contest that gives away only one prize. This is a quick road to contest burnout.

☒ Don't get scammed! If you've won a contest you haven't entered—beware! If you have to be earning $40,000 a year and are required to attend a sales presentation—think twice!

☒ Don't send money to receive a prize—*ever*.

Reprinted with permission from the August 2001 Reader's Digest Canada.

The website address and mailing address listed in the article for the Canadian Contests Newsletter have since changed to:

www.canadiancontests.com

Canadian Contests Newsletter
P.O. Box 23066, RPO McGillivray
Winnipeg, MB R3T 5S3

NOTE: See section, Newsletters, to find American equivalent sweepstakes newsletters you can subscribe to.

I began my sweeping hobby by surfing the web and discovering an entire community of people who enjoy entering sweepstakes. I joined a few groups, signed up for a couple of newsletters and through trial and error came up with an Internet-based sweepstakes entering system that really *works*. How do I know my system works? My results, of course—I consistently win 5-15+ sweeps every month, month after month. I even had a month where I won *83 prizes!*

I am so passionate about sweeping and excited about winning, I decided to write this book after the 100th person asked me what my secret was to winning so much. I knew I was onto something with the system I had developed over the past few years and I wanted to share my discoveries, ideas, thoughts and enthusiasm with others.

Then someone asked me, "Why would you give all your secrets away? Wouldn't teaching others how to be successful sweepers decrease your odds of winning?" It was a tough question…

I was contemplating whether or not I should continue to write the book while driving to a friend's house. On the way I passed a church. The service announcement board out front said "You Can't Lose Helping Others Win." That clinched it—I thought, "That message is for me! God is telling me it is OK to write the book!"

In this book, I will cover everything from how I began, the ins and outs of the five ways to enter sweepstakes, the Internet Sweeping System I have developed over years of entering (and entering and entering…), stories from fellow sweepers, and what pitfalls to avoid along with many tips and tricks to increase your odds of winning.

In the past, most books on the hobby of sweeping focused on only three methods of entering; in-person, phone-in and mail-in. This left out the field of Internet and mobile phone contests, both of which are the newest, fastest growing, and easiest way to enter forms of sweepstakes available today. This book focuses on the Internet/online method of entering sweepstakes. When I began entering sweepstakes on a daily basis there was no single source of sweepstaking information in Canada. My goal is to make this book (and the online resources on my website—www.contestqueen.com) a hub of all the sweepstaking resources available today in North America. With all this information at your fingertips, you can choose which methods of entry you want to participate in, which groups and forums you may want to join, and what types of sweepstakes you want to enter.

I feel sweeping is one of the best, most rewarding hobbies around and I am sure you will feel the same way after your first win. By reading this book and using the many ideas, tips and tricks included within, you can enjoy the hobby of sweeping as much as I do.

NOTE: Occasionally I may use the word contestor in this book. In Canada we use the word contest interchangeably with the word sweepstakes even though by definition they are different. (See section, Promotion Types.)

con·testor (kŏn′tĕst′ər)

n.   1.   One who enters contests, sweepstakes, competitions, lotteries and raffles.

NOTE: You may have noticed that I have spelled the word contestor with an OR as opposed to an ER. There is a reason for this. I created the word contestor because the proper definition of a contester is someone who is protesting or disputing something. We're trying to win cars and big-screen TVs here, not contest a will!

con·testing (kŏn′tĕst′)

v.   1.   The act of entering contests.

con·test (kŏn′tĕst′)

n.   1.   A struggle for superiority or victory between rivals.

2.   A competition, especially one in which entrants perform separately and are rated by judges. See Synonyms at <u>conflict</u>.

con·test·ed, con·test·ing, con·tests (kən′tĕst′) (kŏn′tĕst′)

v. tr.   1.   To compete or strive for.

2.   To call into question and take an active stand against; dispute or challenge: **contest a will.** See Synonyms at <u>oppose</u>.

v. intr.   1.   To struggle or compete; contend: **contested with** other bidders for the antique.

Probably from French *conteste*, from *contester*, to dispute, from Old French, to call to witness, from Latin *contestari* : *com-*, com- + *testis*, *witness*; see trei —in Appendix I.

con·test′a·ble *adj.*

con·tes·ta′tion (kŏn′tĕ-stā′shən) *n.*

11

con·test´er *n.*

con·tes·tant (kən-těs´tənt, kŏn´těs´tənt)

n.   1.   One taking part in a contest; a competitor.

         2.   One that contests or disputes something, such as an election or a will.

Copyright © 2006 by Houghton Mifflin Company. Adapted and reproduced by permission from the *American Heritage Dictionary of the English Language, Fourth Edition.*

sweep·staker (sweep/stāk/ər)

n.   1.   One who enters sweepstakes, contests, competitions, lotteries, and raffles in order to win prizes.

sweeper (sweep/ər)

slang for sweepstaker

n.   1.   One who enters sweepstakes, contests, competitions, lotteries, and raffles in order to win prizes.

sweeping (sweep/ɪŋ)

v.   1.   The act of entering sweepstakes.

Profession or Hobby?

pro·fes·sion·al (prə-fěsh/ə-nəl)

adj.   1.   a.   Of, relating to, engaged in, or suitable for a profession: lawyers, doctors, and other professional people.

             b.   Conforming to the standards of a profession: professional behavior.

        2.   Engaging in a given activity as a source of livelihood or as a career: *a professional writer.*

        3.   Performed by persons receiving pay: *professional football.*

4. Having or showing great skill; expert: *a professional repair job*.

n. 1. A person following a profession, especially a learned profession.

2. One who earns a living in a given or implied occupation: *hired a professional to decorate the house.*

3. A skilled practitioner; an expert.

hob·by (hŏb′ē)

n. pl.   **hob·bies** An activity or interest pursued outside one's regular occupation and engaged in primarily for pleasure.

Copyright © 2006 by Houghton Mifflin Company. Adapted and reproduced by permission from the *American Heritage Dictionary of the English Language, Fourth Edition.*

What is an enthusiastic sweeper called? I have been called a professional sweeper. The term makes me uncomfortable because a professional is an expert in a specific field and is usually well paid for their skill and knowledge. I consider sweeping to be a hobby because 1) it is not my occupation, 2) I do it for pleasure, and 3) I certainly could not live off my winnings.

There are several terms used globally to describe someone who enters sweepstakes on a regular basis. In Canada we refer to ourselves as contestors because we enter contests. In the United States you refer to yourselves as sweepers because you enter sweepstakes. (If we did that in Canada, people would think we were curlers!) In the United Kingdom and Australia they refer to themselves as competitors because they enter competitions. As Shakespeare said, "A rose by any other name would smell as sweet." My favorite term to describe my hobby is *winner*!

MY WINNING STREAK

On a very cold gray day in January, I got the email that every sweeper waits for: Congratulations! Your name has been drawn for the **Grand**

Prize, Trip for two to L.A. and dinner with/prepared by Bob Blumer, in **Meyer's "The Surreal Meal" contest**, sponsored by Alliance Atlantis Broadcasting Inc. and Meyer Canada Inc. (Along with the trip to Los Angeles, I received an eight piece set of Meyer Anolon cookware and $500 spending money.)

TIP: You can collect frequent flyer points on the flights you have won. Each person must have their own account to maximize the free rewards on top of a win.

Craig and I arranged to take the trip in March. We arrived at the airport on Thursday morning and met our chaperone from Alliance Atlantis. (They need to ensure that their show's hosts are protected from crazy sweepers.) It had been a slow month and I had not won a single thing. We got to L.A. and discovered we had two phone messages; one from my Dad and one from my stepmother. Due to the time difference I could not call until Friday morning. When I called, my stepmother said "Are you sitting down?" I was expecting bad news. She then proceeded to tell me my niece won a trip for four to New York City!

At the beginning of the year I told my stepsister, I was going to start entering my niece and nephew in sweepstakes for children. I thought they would enjoy receiving a neat new toy or DVD in the mail. Little did I know their first win would be "a big one!" (I consider it my win even though I didn't get the prize because I did the entering.) I was so happy for them since they had never been on a family vacation and they were now going on the trip of a lifetime.

We then proceeded to have an amazing time in Los Angeles. We arrived at Bob's home in the Hollywood Hills at 8:00pm on Friday evening. He had called me a few weeks before the trip to discuss the menu. We agreed he would make us recipes from his upcoming cookbook *Surreal Gourmet Bites: show-stoppers and conversation starters*. Bob is also an oenophile so each course was paired with a selection from his extensive private wine collection. He is a wonderful host. Craig and I felt as if we had gone to a friend's home for dinner. I went out and purchased his new book when it was released so I could continue to enjoy his creations and share them with my family and friends.

14

NOTE: There are no photos of our evening with Bob in this book. It is important to read all the documents you sign with regards to a sweepstakes win. The sweepstakes prize waiver stated all photos taken during our evening are for personal use only and cannot be published. I can publish other photos of us taken that weekend.

We arrived home late Sunday night, tired, happy and feeling lucky that we had such a memorable long weekend. As a sweeper you never know how long a dry spell will last or how long a winning streak will continue. At 10:00am Monday morning Craig got a phone call from a local radio station. He won a two-week European holiday—a nine country, fourteen day bus tour. He was shocked.

We went to Europe that September. The trip was with a tour company that specialized in youth groups 18-35. It was fast paced and had a party atmosphere. Being up late every night, getting up early every morning and running around a new city almost daily took its toll on me by the end of the vacation. I came home with a terrible cold, having sadly discovered I wasn't 21 anymore and couldn't keep up the pace I used to. No wonder they say 18-35! It's really tough on those of us over 35.

TIP: If one half of the couple is under 35 and the other is over, the older person can sign a waiver stating you understand the tour is designed for "young" people.

We visited London, Amsterdam, the Rhine Valley, Munich, Innsbruck, Hofgarten, Venice, Rome, Florence, Lucerne, Paris and then back to London. What a vacation! The two surprise bonuses of the tour were arriving in Munich on opening day of Oktoberfest (Who knew Oktoberfest started in September?) and seeing the last 10 minutes of Pope John Paul II's Wednesday morning sermon in Rome.

The highlight of the vacation for me was the evening trip up the Eiffel Tower. I have always wanted to go to Paris, and standing on the upper deck, hugging Craig and looking over the lights of Paris as the tower twinkled was absolutely magical. I felt so lucky!

Our best adventure on the tour was the morning we had a $100 breakfast. It was the second last day of the trip and we were in Paris. After a brief tour of a perfumery, we found ourselves outside of the Opera House. We were hungry and decided to have a bite to eat, and were tired of eating small, quick breakfasts. Looking around we noticed Le Café de la Paix, Paris' most famous restaurant. (Embarrassingly, I did not recognize the name. Craig did recognize the name, remembering many world famous chefs began their careers in that very café.) We entered from the street entrance and I was thinking we might sit outside. Craig and I discussed our eating options with the Maitre D', and decided we would like to have the breakfast buffet.

They sat us inside in a booth opposite the hotel entrance. As we waited for our tea and coffee to arrive we noticed several very well dressed people come into the restaurant.

Then we went to the buffet. I have never seen a buffet like this in my life! There were breads and cheeses from all over the world, twenty different kinds of fresh fruit, four types of fresh fruit juice, and the best scrambled eggs I have ever eaten. They even had an entire section of Japanese specialties. When I came back to the table I said to Craig, "I don't think we want to know what breakfast is going to cost us." We sat for an hour relaxing, eating, and deciding what were going to see that afternoon and soaking in the atmosphere. When the bill arrived it was €64 ($100). It was worth every penny!

Many people ask me when I have time to enter so many sweepstakes. I have to quote R.J. Ward from a sign we found in the Tinker Town Museum just outside Santa Fe, NM:

You Can't Win If You Don't Enter

NOTE: All the web addresses, URLs, and other contact details listed in this book were correct at press time. The Internet is very fluid and URLs, websites, web page and emails change daily. We consistently post all changes and updates on our website at www.contestqueen.com.

WHY RUN A SWEEPSTAKES?

One question I get asked frequently is, "Do companies really give away all those prizes? It must be a scam."

Yes, they really do give away those prizes.

No one runs a sweepstakes because they are feeling generous. Sweepstakes are a way for companies to attract or keep customers, pure and simple. They use our desire for the prize as a lure to get us to buy their products and services or expose ourselves to their advertising message. The advantage to the company is that the lure of the prize will keep customers' attention longer than other forms of advertising—we *want* what they are giving away, and are willing to endure their message or buy more of a product or service than we normally would to give ourselves a better chance of winning.

Companies build sweepstakes into their total marketing and advertising annual budget because sweepstakes are fun way to get a consumer involved with their product or service. In 2007, companies in the U.S. spent $1.89 billion running sweepstakes. There are a lot of legitimate prizes to be won!

Companies run sweepstakes for a variety of specific reasons. They hold sweepstakes to:

- attract attention to their brand, product or service;
- increase sales;
- maintain or increase customer loyalty;
- increase their customer database;

- begin permission marketing. (You say it's OK for them to send you something via email or mail.)

A company needs to determine what it wants to accomplish and design a simple sweepstakes around that purpose.

If you ever feel a sweepstakes is confusing, complicated or unfair, contact the company promoting the sweepstakes (the judging agency or sweepstakes management company, the sponsor, or both) and ask for clarification of what you are finding frustrating. I have seen many sweepstakes change the entry page or the rules mid-promotion period, based on contestant feedback. Unfortunately, some companies make sweepstakes so complicated the original purpose of running the sweepstakes is defeated.

STORY: Susan submitted a good story on how some companies miss the point of a promotion (to create product or service awareness and attract new customers) by making the sweepstakes too confusing or difficult to enter.

℮ℭ

Susan—Rose Bay, NS
A few months ago they had a sweepstakes in the local paper and you also had to listen to the local radio station for a daily clue letter. This went on for several weeks and my sister and I faithfully got each letter. They didn't have any letters for the weekends. If you didn't hear the letter, you could go to the local mall and the letters would be posted at the lotto booth. (It's 30 minute drive away for me.) You also had to cut four parts of a computer picture out of the local weekly paper (one each week for four weeks) and paste them on to the entry form. My other sister wanted to enter too, so she went to friends and got their old papers, since she and my mother share the paper.

When the sweepstakes was over you had a week to put your entries in. It only took my sister and I a few hours to figure out the phrase, KNOWLEDGE PAYS, from the letters given. I took my mom's entry out with mine. My other two sisters took their entry forms in separately.

At the end of the sweepstakes my mom got a call that she had won the computer, printer, camera and scanner. When I went to take Mom to collect her prize, we ended up chatting with the girl in the lotto booth (where the letters were posted), and she said the sweepstakes must have been too complicated as there were only eight entries. Great odds!!

Needless to say, my nephew (who lives with my mom most of the time) is in Grade 5 and it didn't take him long to hook up the computer. I wasn't there to see his eyes light up but I know he was thrilled to be able to do his homework on the computer. My mom, who is 70, still doesn't know much about it but wouldn't sell it and it's not hooked up to the Internet. What a wonderful win.

ഇൗങ്ങ

The premise of the promotion was to use multiple mass media vehicles and get people to participate. However, it was so difficult and cumbersome that most people were scared away or couldn't be bothered to enter resulting in only eight entries.

TIP: If a sweepstakes seems complicated, don't let it discourage you from entering. As Susan found, you might not have many other entries to compete against, which will increase your chances of winning.

PROMOTION TYPES

There is a difference between a lottery, a contest and a sweepstakes. It is important to understand the differences because it could determine what types of promotions you prefer to enter.

Lotteries and Sweepstakes Versus Contests

You're probably aware of the words "lotteries," "sweepstakes," and "contests," but you may not really understand how they differ from one another. This section will discuss their differences, as well and their relative advantages and disadvantages.

It's easier to define sweepstakes and contests by starting with their more familiar grandfather: the lottery. A lottery is any game that consists of three elements. These three elements are chance (luck), the entry fee (sometimes referred to as the "consideration"), and the prize. The first element—

luck—is introduced by the very fact that you're competing against thousands of other people by predicting several numbers that will be chosen at random. The entry fee is generally the price of the ticket itself. Most lottery tickets cost one dollar. And the prizes are usually money.

What differentiates a sweepstakes or contest from a lottery is that one of these three elements has been removed. In a sweepstakes, that element is the entry fee. In other words, the game is still a game of chance, and there are still prizes to be won (although not necessarily cash prizes), but you don't have to pay to enter.

Contests retain the entry fee but remove the luck as a determining factor. The entry fee is usually in the form of purchasing one or more of the company's products. For example, a contest often requires you to send in a proof of purchase or label. Obviously, you cannot obtain these items without buying the product. It doesn't matter whether you personally bought it or one of your friends purchased it. The luck is removed by adding an element of skill. Whereas sweepstakes are determined through random drawings, contests require the participants to perform in some way. A contest may ask you to write a song or create a rhythm, or explain why you use a product. A panel of judges determines which contestant has demonstrated the most skill.

People tend to believe contests are more legitimate because they're sometimes required to pay an entry fee. One reason companies like contests so much is that they are another way of generating affordable advertising. Not only does the contest itself increase consumer interest, but the company might end up with a catchy slogan or jingle for its product when the contest is over. This slogan might just be as good as one created by a professional marketing firm, and the prize given to the winner is likely to be less expensive than hiring such a firm.

***How to Win Lotteries, Sweepstakes and Contests in the 21st Century* by Steve Ledoux. Copyright ©2004 Santa Monica Press LLC. Used by permission of Santa Monica Press LLC, 800-784-9553, www.santamonicapress.com.**

Lotteries

There are several different types of lotteries: jackpot draws (Powerball), daily draws (Big 4), and instant games (scratch and win) for example.

Information regarding each state's lotteries can be located at the following websites. The websites are quite comprehensive and have everything from winning numbers to Frequently Asked Questions regarding each lottery.

NOTE: If a state is not listed, they do not offer lotteries.

Arizona
www.arizonalottery.com

California
www.calottery.com

Colorado
www.coloradolottery.com

Connecticut
www.ctlottery.org

Delaware
http://lottery.state.de.us

District of Columbia
www.dclottery.com

Florida
www.flalottery.com

Georgia
www.galottery.com

Idaho
www.idaholottery.com

Illinois
www.illinoislottery.com

Indiana
www.hoosierlottery.com

Iowa
www.ialottery.com

Kansas
www.kslottery.com

Kentucky
www.kylottery.com

Louisiana
www.louisianalottery.com

Maine
www.mainelottery.com

Maryland
www.mdlottery.com

Massachusetts
www.masslottery.com

Michigan
www.michigan.gov/lottery

Minnesota
www.mnlottery.com

Missouri
www.molottery.com

Montana
www.montanalottery.com

Nebraska
www.nelottery.com

New Hampshire
www.nhlottery.com

New Jersey
www.njlottery.net

New Mexico
www.nmlottery.com

New York
www.nylottery.org

North Carolina
www.nc-educationlottery.org

North Dakota
www.ndlottery.org

Ohio
www.ohiolottery.com

Oklahoma
www.lottery.ok.gov

Oregon
www.oregonlottery.org

Pennsylvania
www.palottery.state.pa.us

Rhode Island
www.rilot.com

South Carolina
www.sceducationlottery.com

South Dakota
www.sdlottery.org

Tennessee
www.tnlottery.com

Texas
www.txlottery.org

Vermont
www.vtlottery.com

West Virginia
www.wvlottery.com

Virginia
www.valottery.com

Wisconsin
www.wilottery.com

Washington
www.walottery.com

Multi-State Lottery Association (www.musl.com) is entirely owned and operated by the member lotteries offering the games.

North American Association of State and Provincial Lotteries (www.naspl.org) is an organization whose purpose is to be a hub of information for its members.

Sweepstakes

The main focus of this book is sweepstakes, including the promotions I discuss, the methods of entry, and my Internet Sweeping System. When I meet fellow sweepers online or post to one of the sweepstaking discussion groups, it is usually about a sweepstakes. This is because sweepstakes, in general, require the least amount of effort to enter and can reap a great reward. You just need to fill out an entry form, submit it and hope you win. Most of the promotions I enter are sweepstakes. I enter a few contests and, on occasion, I buy lottery tickets.

Contests

There are all types of contests you can enter: cooking, baking, woodworking, writing and photography, to name just a few. These are great to enter because the number of entrants is usually quite low due to the extra "skill" work involved compared to sweepstakes (with the exception of the Annual Pillsbury Bake Off which garners thousands of entries). So, if you have a particular hobby, skill or talent, look for contests where you can not only enjoy what you are doing (e.g. taking photographs, writing poetry or inventing new recipes) you can also possibly win cash and/or prizes doing it.

Ironically, I rarely enter essay and story-based contests. Let me explain. These types of contests are usually judged on the best story. I may write well, however, I feel I usually do not have a story good enough to win. I do enter many cooking and baking contests because cooking and baking are another love of mine. For example, my chili recipe won 3rd prize in a Super Bowl of Chili Cook Off in 2002.

Carolyn's Award-Winning Awesome Chicken Chili

3lbs. ground chicken (I prefer to grind my own using skinless boneless thighs.)
1 large Spanish onion, diced
1 tbsp. canola oil
4 large or 6 medium tomatoes, diced (a can of diced tomatoes can be used if desired)
1 green pepper, seeded and diced
1 red pepper, seeded and diced
1 yellow pepper, seeded and diced
1 orange pepper, seeded and diced
1 cubanelle pepper, seeded and diced
1 hot banana pepper, seeded and diced
1 jalapeno pepper, seeded and diced
1 chili pepper, seeded and finely diced (use gloves for this step, trust me!)
1 tbsp. chili powder*
1 tbsp. hot chili flakes*
10 dashes of Tabasco
1 tsp. salt*
1 tsp. ground black pepper*
1 19oz. can black beans, drained and rinsed
1 19oz. can kidney beans, drained and rinsed

This is one of the easiest recipes ever. I place all the ingredients (except for the oil, the onion and the chicken) in to an 8qt. pot and turn the heat on low. In a cold frying pan pour in the oil and turn the heat on medium low (the cooking temperatures were determined by my halogen stove top and may be adjusted for your stove). Once the oil is hot, turn the

heat to low, put the onion in the pan, sauté until soft, and then add the onion to the pot. In the same frying pan, place the raw chicken (add a bit more oil if it is required) and cook until there is no pink color left. (I find the chicken browns faster if I put the lid on the frying pan.) Drain the chicken and then add the chicken to the pot. Stir about every ½ hour. Put the lid on until the chili boils then I find the chili turns out best if cooked on low without a lid for 3-4 hours. Otherwise, there is too much liquid and it is too runny to scoop with chips.
*to taste

My prize for such a delicious recipe was a nice basket of Tabasco branded goodies including an apron, a golf shirt, a silk scarf and enough Tabasco sauce to make a ton of chili!

I also collect cookbooks. My father purchased an old box at an auction, in the box was *The Nellie Aldridge Cook Book—Many Ways to Utilize the Citrus Fruits of the San Bernardo Valley.* The book is undated. Inside is a wonderful example of a contest entry from days gone-by.

Orange Sunshine Cake
Whites of 10 eggs, yolks of 6 eggs; 1 cup granulated sugar, 1 teaspoon flavoring, 1 cup Swan's Down cake Flour, 1 teaspoon cream of tartar. Beat whites of eggs until stiff and dry, add sugar gradually and continue beating; then add yolks of eggs beaten until thick and lemon colored, and 1 teaspoon orange extract. Cut and fold in flour mixed and sifted with cream of tartar. Bake 60 minutes in a slow oven*, in an angel cake pan.

In a cake baking contest held by Misses Hancock and Wade of the Home Furniture Company of San Bernardino this cake scored 98½ points winning a $55.00 Acorn Gas Range, given as a prize for the best cake.
*A slow oven is 300°F.

NOTE: There is a difference between a contest that wants you to submit a story (e.g. why your mom is the best) and a sweepstakes' no purchase entry option asking you to submit your entry along with a 25-50 word essay. The contest winner will be selected by a panel of judges and the sweepstakes winner will be drawn at random. Therefore, even if you feel you don't not have the best creative writing skills, and wouldn't enter the contest, enter the sweepstakes as your writing skills will not be judged.

*Anybody can win unless there
happens to be a second entry."
George Ade*

THE OFFICIAL RULES

My #1 tip:
**Read The Official Rules
and Follow Them!**

This is my number one tip because most people don't read the official rules. One company I interviewed said only 2% of the people clicked the Official Rules button on online sweepstakes entry pages. Another source stated that up to 40% of mail-in entries were disqualified because the official rules were not followed.

It is <u>very important</u> to read the Official Rules to see:

- if you are eligible to enter;
- how many times you can enter;
- how many people in the household can enter;
- the start and end dates of the sweepstakes;
- any other rules specific to that sweepstakes.

I have potentially disqualified myself countless times by not reading the rules before I enter. I have entered:

- out-of-state or out-of-country sweepstakes;
- more than once in a one-entry-per-person sweepstakes;
- both my husband and myself in one-entry-per-household sweepstakes;
- before the sweepstakes starts;
- my husband in women only sweepstakes;
- sweepstakes where I did not meet the age requirements.

Many sweepstakes have overlapping methods of entry. Reading the official rules will also allow you to determine the best entry method for you.

> All sweepstakes must have official rules, which is the contract between the sponsor of the sweepstakes and people that are eligible to enter. The official rules CANNOT change once the rules have been published and entries have been accepted.

> The official rules must typically contain the following information: 1) A no purchase is necessary statement; 2) start and end dates; 3) eligibility requirements (age, residency, also specify exclusions); 4) methods of entry – including a "no purchase" method of entry; 5) any limitations on the number of entries by a single person or household; 6) odds of winning; 7) description and value of the prize(s); 8) how the winner(s) will be selected and notified; 9) restrictions on receiving the prize; and 10) sponsor's name and address. Additional disclosures are required depending on the type of promotion and the jurisdictions and channels in which it is offered. Internet promotions may trigger other additional requirements.

> **Courtesy of The Lustigman Firm, P.C., 212-683-9180, www.sweepstakeslaw.com or www.lfirm.com**

Each state has varying laws governing sweepstakes. Gambling lawyer Chuck Humphrey, of Gambling-Law-US, created a wonderful online resource of U.S. gambling laws. Visit www.gambling-law-us.com/State-Laws/. Click on each state to read the text of these laws, including the full text of any specific sweepstakes laws. (See section, *Government Regulations*.)

I Didn't Read the Rules

I received a very exciting email one day informing me that I had won a trip to Santa Fe and Taos, New Mexico. Then I read the fine print: I had only won the hotel stay. Airfare and car rental were not included. What was I thinking?! Why would I enter a sweepstakes that wasn't all inclusive? Apparently, I had not read the rules very carefully. I looked up the hotels on the Internet. They looked very nice. The hotel stay was worth quite a bit. Hmmm…what to do, what to do?! I talked it over with my husband and we decided to go. Luckily for us we had enough airline points saved up so we cashed them in for the airfare and part of the car rental. New Mexico was not a holiday destination I would normally think of. We had a great time and I highly recommend going if you are looking for somewhere new to visit. The landscape was gorgeous, the food was fantastic and the people were wonderful. Craig and I would like to go back.

Since we had enough points saved to cover airfare and car rentals, this story had a happy ending. It could have cost us a pretty penny or I may have had to turn down the prize. You can be sure that now, I always read the rules thoroughly. Sometimes I even read them twice!

I will repeat my #1 sweeping tip because it is so important:
Read The Official Rules *and* Follow Them!

You Can't Win If You Don't Enter

"Luck is believing you're lucky."
Tennessee Williams

FIVE WAYS TO ENTER

There are five ways a company will allow entries into their sweepstakes:

- in-store/in-person;
- radio/phone-in;
- mail-in;
- online/Internet;
- text messaging (cell phone).

You will notice as you read a sweepstakes' official rules that sometimes you can enter using more than one of the entry methods or that they have been combined to give you one entry. An example of alternative entry methods would be entering either by mail *or* online. An example of combined entry methods would be to text-in an entry *that gives you* a code to enter online.

The secret to the hobby of sweepstaking is to make it your own. It is meant to be fun, not work. Try different entry methods, visit various websites, subscribe to a few newsletters, etc. Find what you like, what makes you feel good (see chapter, *Attracting Luck*), and what brings in wins for you. Everyone could use more dreams, fun and excitement in their lives.

NOTE: There are more resources available than I could possibly write about in this book. Included are the people, companies, websites, groups and forums that wished to participate in this book. The Internet is also a very "fluid" place and websites come and go in a heartbeat. Remember to check www.contestqueen.com under Resources for additional and frequently updated sweepstaking resources.

IN-STORE

In-store sweepstakes are either: a fill-in entry form sweepstakes, a game piece collection style promotion or a seeded sweepstakes.

The entry form style of promotion is designed to draw in foot traffic and potential sales into the store or near the product sponsoring the promotion, as well as to expand the store's mailing list. They are usually found at the front of the store or near the cash register. The odds in this type of promotion are usually good since many times the prize is one per store, the entry period is short, it has not been advertised to the general public and the people that do enter, generally only fill out one entry form.

TIP: Do not help yourself to the entire entry pad, fill the entry forms out at home and then go back to the store to enter them. The sweepstakes may have unlimited entries, however, it is on the edge of cheating and it is not good karma, (see chapter, Attracting Luck).

If the rules are available, it is important to read them. If a major retail chain is holding the entry form method of drawing, the rules are usually printed on the back of the entry form or posted near the entry box. Major retailers have been known to limit entries to one entry per person or one entry per household for the entire chain. They also do not necessarily pool all the entry forms together. I have seen promotions where the entries are filled out country wide, and then a particular store is chosen; a name is then selected from the entry box in that specific store. Another method is a few entry forms from each store are sent to the company's head office, and the winner is selected from those entry forms only.

Game sweepstakes originally were only conducted with the in-store method of entry. With the advent of Internet sweepstakes, some game sweepstakes now involve purchasing or mailing away for PIN codes (Personal Identification Number) or game pieces to be entered on a specific online sweepstakes website.

NOTE: PIN code based sweepstakes are being run more frequently by sponsor companies because it makes it easy for the average consumer to enter once while at the same time making it harder for those that make a habit of entering multiple times.

Game sweepstakes are the fastest growing form of sweepstakes today. The major reason for their popularity is that a sweepstakes player participates in finding out whether or not he or she has won a prize.

Some sweepstakes players view game sweepstakes as the fast food version of "regular" sweepstakes—they remove some of the mystery from sweepstakes. In random draw sweepstakes, one fills out and submits an entry, not certain whether the entry will win or lose. Players are only notified later if they win. There is no way to know whether you have lost a sweepstakes unless you request a winners list. (We've never heard of a judging organization that notifies the losers.)

In game sweepstakes, the number of prizes and the number of entries are predetermined. The number of entries is determined by the number of game pieces printed. (Only a fixed percentage of the total number of game pieces printed are winners.) The number of people playing a game sweepstakes has no effect on your chances of winning. Either you get a winning card or you do not.

Not all game sweepstakes are the same. There are five types of game sweepstakes: collect, match, decode and instant-win predetermined and instant-win probability.

Collect. To win the collect game sweepstakes, the entrant must collect game pieces (of which usually one is rare) to spell a word, build a picture, and so forth. Many potential players unwittingly discard the rare piece.

Match. Match game sweepstakes usually involve matching a number or picture from a game piece to a list of winning selections. Typically, the winning selections are posted in retail stores, or can be obtained through the mail.

Decode. Decode game sweepstakes usually instruct the entrant to take his or her game piece to a special

35

decoding display in a store to see if it is a winner. The game pieces are always scrambled so that it cannot be read without the "special" decoder. Some new fangled decode sweepstakes require computer equipment to play. In 1989 K Mart put bar codes on store flyers which customers brought to K Mart stores to be scanned. The computer announced if and what the customer won.

Instant-Win Predetermined. Predetermined instant-win sweepstakes usually feature a game piece from which you scratch off a covering layer, which reveals any prize that may have been won. For example, in scratching a card three panels may be revealed; if all match, the card is a winner. How you scratch the game piece has no affect because the outcome is predetermined.

It is sometimes possible to differentiate winning and losing game pieces prior to playing if the pieces were printed separately. One can look for slight differences such as a filled in letter "e" or a stray dot that might appear only on winning game pieces.

Instant-Win Probability. In probability games, every piece is a potential winner if scratched or played properly. For example, Applian Way Pizza ran a probability instant-win game in which ten spots were covered with a film layer. Two of the ten spots carried matching prizes. If the player could uncover the matching spots with only two scratches, he or she won the prize indicated. Every game card was a potential winner of $5 to $5,000.

Copyright ©1990 by Jeffrey & Robin Sklar. Extract from *Winning Sweepstakes* published by Sebell Publishing Company Inc.

I always support the sweepstakes sponsor by buying their products to get the PIN codes. When companies deem their promotions are successful, they will keep running them and possibly, even run more.

However, it is not healthy to eat too much chocolate, soda pop, sugary cereal, etc. In addition to buying the sponsor's products, I use the No Purchase Entry (NPE) method and send away for additional PIN codes or I go PIN code hunting.

In the book *The Prize Winner of Defiance Ohio*, Dortha Schaefer takes Evelyn Ryan to the city dump to get "qualies" (Qualifiers such as labels, box tops, UPCs, etc.) I am not that ambitious, but every week I used to pass many product containers with PIN codes on them in blue bins on recycle day and think to myself, "Look at all those winning opportunities just being thrown away!" Now I don't let those potential wins go to waste. Weather permitting, on recycle day I take a walk around my neighborhood. I take along a plastic bag to collect the soda pop bottle lids and a pair of scissors to cut off any codes on bottles or boxes. Not only am I getting exercise, but I am possibly collecting the trip of a lifetime, a big screen TV or a new car!

TIP: Get your family and friends to help you win. One of our sweepstakes club members finds a bag of "garbage" outside her door once a week. Her neighbor saves anything with a PIN code on it and gives it to her since they do not enter. In return she passes back little wins such as movie passes or CDs.

Most promotions have a NPE option where you can send away for a free package sample, PIN code, entry form, etc. Legally, the odds are the same if you bought the product or send away for a NPE.

STORY: Aimee proved you can win fantastic prizes from sending away for the NPE.

ℴ⇣

Aimee—Baldwinsville, NY
Libby's ran a sweeps called Labels for Laptops. The rules were very specific. To enter you had to mail-in five papers with the name of Libby's vegetables, all written in blue ink, to receive a scratch card. I sent away for 64 scratch cards!! Everyday religiously I put on my I AM Lucky essential oil and I kept picturing myself winning one of those laptops. After spending, what felt like hours, fruitlessly scratching those little cards, on my last card, the 64th, I won a laptop!!

ℴ⇣

Seeded sweepstakes are the hardest to win because it involves finding the winning piece in thousands or even millions of product containers (e.g. bottle cap liners, toilet rolls, talking cans, etc.). Charlie and the Chocolate Factory (by Ronald Dahl) is a fictional example of a seeded sweepstakes. The children had to be lucky enough to find a golden ticket in the chocolate bar packaging to win an invitation to the chocolate factory.

NOTE: There is a difference between collect-to-win and seeded sweepstakes even though both have very rare winning pieces, coupons, notifications, etc. In the collect-to-win you get a game piece(s) with every purchase and you hope you get one of the rare winning pieces. In seeded sweepstakes you do not collect anything. You just hope you are lucky enough to find the winning certificate, notification, etc.

Second Chance Drawings

Sponsors often hold second chance drawings to award unclaimed prizes once their primary promotion has closed. Not every promotion will hold a second chance drawing, so it is important to read the rules to determine how the judging agency will be handling any unclaimed prizes.

Second chance drawings are usually held in conjunction with instant win sweepstakes which include: instant win games in which you scratch a card and you are told immediately if you won (either a physical card or virtual card, online), collect and win games (where you collect game pieces to complete a certain set) and match and win games (where you match a symbol or word to a posted list of winners).

Once the promotion is over, many sponsors still want to award those prizes which were not claimed during the regular promotional period. Only about 30% of the prizes are awarded in an instant win promotion. The sponsoring company counts on the low claim rate because even if they are awarding the larger prizes in a second chance drawing, they do not have to award all the prizes. This allows them to either: 1) offer larger prizes on a smaller promotional marketing budget or 2) leaving enough funds in their marketing budget to run another instant win sweepstakes.

This is why, in most cases, these second chance entries are the easiest to win. There are usually large prize pools left over to be given away. The prizes go unclaimed for the following reasons:

- they are still sitting on the store shelf after the promotional period has ended;
- the product has been purchased, but is sitting in the pantry of someone's home;
- the product was purchased, but the game pieces were tossed in the trash by a non-sweeper;
- the game piece was checked, but misplaced or tossed out in error.

TIP: Look around when eating at a fast food restaurant, a ballgame or the movies. How many cups, bottles, bags or boxes are left around with the games pieces still intact? They will end up in the trash if not collected by someone, so go claim those winning opportunities for yourself!

When you see a sweepstakes offering a second chance drawing, immediately check to see how many prizes will be available at the end of the promotion if any are left unclaimed. In some cases, they only draw names for the unclaimed Grand Prize or largest prizes, such as when the lower level prizes are some of their own products or when they feel they can reuse the products in another promotion at a later date. Only send in one or two entries to the second chance drawing if there are only one or two possible winners in this part of the promotion. If there are a lot of prizes being given away, then send in more entries based either on the amount of possible prizes to be won or your comfort level. I like to send in up to 20 entries depending on the prize, but I know others who will send in hundreds.

NOTE: Just because there are hundreds of prizes being awarded in the main promotion, it doesn't mean there will be hundreds available for the second chance drawing. Again, be sure to read the rules under the Unclaimed Prizes or Second Chance headings in the sponsor's rules. Then make your decision on how many entries to send.

Sometimes you don't need to do anything to enter a second chance drawing. Those entering promotions online and playing interactive games may discover when they lose on the initial step of the promotion that they are automatically entered into a second chance drawing.

TIP: While grocery shopping check the aisles for products that have game pieces or codes inside the packaging. Read the rules and see what the second chance drawing options are and if you wish to enter because in many cases, after the promotion has ended, you will still see sweepstakes labeled products for sale on the shelf, but now invalid because the promotion is over. Therefore, the odds of winning in the second chance drawing may be very good.

I always encourage those new to the hobby to enter the sweepstakes and second chance drawings with lots of prizes being given away. The prizes may not necessarily be big ticket items, but it is a great way to begin to win.

STORY: You are never too young to start entering sweepstakes, raffles or contests.

₧₨

Al—Dearborn, MI
My first entry into entering contests came when I was 12 years old. I lived in Hingham, MA and my father decided to take the whole family on a trip to Portland, ME to see my mother's sister. On the way (we went by train) we stopped over at Old Orchid Beach, ME. They had an amusement park and a beach. We were to stay there for the day and catch the late train to Portland. My mother saw this brand new steam iron (it had just come on the market) and since she did laundry for a living, really wanted it. My father wasn't much of a gambler, so I borrowed $1 from him and bought a chance to win the steam iron. I won the iron and I also won a candy guessing game. That was the start of my interest in entering contests. It wasn't until about 1960 before I began entering contests fairly regularly and I have been sweeping ever since. I'm still looking for a car and I know it is coming.

₧₨

RADIO/PHONE-IN

Radio contests are designed to keep a listener hooked for their next opportunity to call-in and win. When larger prizes are given away, they are designed to keep listeners hooked for days or weeks at a time. You will generally find the larger the market, the better the prizes. This is because in larger cities, they have more listeners; therefore they can charge their advertisers more and have more funds available for bigger promotions. It is usually also more difficult to "get through" on the contest phone line as more people are trying to qualify or win the giveaway.

NOTE: You can listen to many radio stations from around the globe online. Be aware: 1) there is usually minor time delay, a few seconds, between what is aired live on the radio and what is aired over the Internet and 2) many radio stations require you to pick-up your prize in person at the station. If you live in San Francisco, you may enjoy the music from the Chicago radio station but you may be wasting your time trying to win their promotions.

In the past when a radio station gave away a prize you had to be the 7th, 10th, 25th, etc. caller through on the contest phone line to win the prize. As the Internet became more popular, radio stations began to add online sweepstakes as a way to "level the playing field" because if you were terrible at dialing-in, everyone could fill out an online entry form.

More and more radio stations are implementing online loyalty listener clubs in addition to their standard phone-in radio contests and online entry sweepstakes. Listeners can accumulate points by listening for codes then return to the station's website, enter the code and rack up points. Many also have other methods of accumulating points such as online games and trivia for additional club points. With your accumulated points you could bid for prizes or enter into sweepstakes.

There are two caveats you need to be aware of before becoming a member of your favorite radio station's loyalty listener club.

The first being, not all stations' sweepstakes are open to the listeners of only one radio station. Since there are very few independently owned radio stations, the conglomerates are combining their marketing budgets and online efforts. You are now no longer entering sweepstakes competing against those within the immediate listening area, but within all the markets in which the parent company owns radio stations.

You may be able to tell if your radio station's sweepstakes are open to more than one region. Some radio stations code their prizes with either a MM or L. MM means Multiple Market and L means Local. This means if you are entering a sweepstakes to win a prize marked MM you are possibly competing against all loyalty club members for every radio station the parent company owns in the entire country! Remember to read the rules for each sweepstakes before you spend your points "buying" entries so you understand what your odds of winning really are. That said, remember that it only takes one entry to win, no matter how many people enter.

The second caveat is the sharing of codes given out over the radio. These codes are virtually always shared by sweepstakers in online sweepstakes clubs, groups and forums. Most radio stations not only do not like the sharing, some have gone so far as to join the online groups masquerading as sweepstakers and post code words that deduct points. Anyone who uses those code words is then banned from their website forever.

NOTE: Radio stations are frequently able to tell which club members are sharing on-air codes because most people use the same nickname and email address for all of their online sweepstaking activities.

The first sweepstakes I can remember entering was a radio contest to see Burton Cummings at Hamilton Place. I stood in the kitchen for ages dialing on a rotary dial phone hoping to be the fourth caller through. I was so excited when I won those tickets. I was only fourteen so my mom had to go down and pick up the tickets. She also went with me to the concert. We sat fourth row center. I felt so grown-up and so lucky!

With life getting busier and busier, I find I am rarely entering radio call-in contests. I always seem to be driving or on a call when the announcer plays the cue to call-in. At the same time, I know there are many people who have tremendous luck calling-in-to-win.

TIP: Bea had a really good tip on how she "gets through" on her local radio station's contest line. She won a trip to see U2 in Los Angeles. Try this method of entering and decide for yourself if it is for you.

ຮດແ

Bea—Toronto, ON

The redial button on the phone that I qualified on is really fast. I have a cordless phone and another phone that is more expensive but slow in redialing. The main suggestion I have is before you hear the cue to call is to start calling. With this contest I had to call after hearing two U2 songs. In between they placed the cue but I literally started a couple seconds before. Never give up. I know that radio call-in contests can be more difficult but be persistent. I was going to give up since I didn't qualify the first weekend. I could hardly believe it when the DJs called me Monday morning to tell me I had won. I had forgotten to set my alarm and literally woke up seconds before the phone rang. We had an awesome time at the concert.

ຮດແ

TIP: To increase your odds of dialing in and getting through, try listening to less popular radio stations.

I did have great luck with one call-in-to-win contest. When my daughter was an infant I was able to call-in to qualify my husband for a 'Guy's Get-Away'. It was 7:00am on a Sunday morning. I was breast-feeding my daughter in front of the computer while I entered sweepstakes online. In the background I had the radio on listening for my cue to call-in. When I heard the signal, I dialed right away. I was caller one. I thought, "Darn, I dialed too fast." Then I thought, "I should try again." I was caller two. I looked at the phone puzzled. I called back. I was caller three, four, five and six! I don't think anyone else was listening at that hour. I knew then we were going to win. Since

it was a male oriented prize I gave the announcer my husband's name.

The next morning was the big draw. I was up at 5:00am feeding my daughter and heard which DJ was announcing that morning. Then I went

43

back to bed turning the ringer on our phone back on. (It had been turned off since our daughter had been born.) At 7:10am the phone rang. I picked it up and sure enough it was the DJ. I screamed "WE WON! WE WON!" shaking awake my sound asleep husband. He sat up bewildered and I handed him the phone. They confirmed it was Craig and told him he was going to Florida to be a judge in the Miss Hawaiian Tropics Bikini Contest State Finals. We had a ball. I don't think we could have fit any more fun into three days. All his friends wanted to know where they could find a wife like me (or like the bikini models!).

STORY: Radio stations run fantastic promotions that involve their listeners allowing them to possibly participate in an adventure.

⁂

Joe—Colona, IL
Two DJs from our local radio station hold an annual Adult Easter Egg Hunt. I usually cannot attend because they hold it on the morning of Good Friday and I work. In 1998, I had the opportunity because I was off work. That year they had one egg containing $1000. When I showed up they had 1000 Easter Eggs scattered on a football field and was putting those of us who were going after them around the outside of the field.

They started to announce the rules, stating that there were over 2000 people surrounding the field and only 1000 eggs so there would be some people who would not receive an egg. They said that in five minutes they would fire a cannon, and at that sound we could go after the eggs.

I told my friends, Diana, Mike, and Patti to look around at all the people. They looked like they were so much faster than I was so I had to have a plan if I wanted to get any eggs.

With less than five minutes, I came up with the following plan: I predicted that everyone is going to stop and pick up the first egg they came to so I wouldn't even think about that close egg, I was concentrating on the eggs in the center of the field. Sounds good right?

After what seemed like an eternity, the cannon finally fired and we were off. What I didn't plan on was a couple to my right running while holding hands. They ran into my path and the woman fell pulling the

44

man down with her, right in front of me. With my catlike reactions, I did an OJ Simpson style leap over them. Well, either I didn't quite clear them, or they were already standing up, but I tripped up on his back.

I ended up doing a belly flop onto the ground and scooping eggs in as I slid across the grass. While over a thousand people did not get any eggs, I got five. I didn't get the $1000 egg. Two of my eggs contained candy, one egg had a $20 gift certificate to a grocery store, one egg had a $25 gift certificate to a restaurant and the last egg had $50 cash in it. Not bad for a guy who doesn't have to stuff his Santa suit.

ᏝᏋ

MAIL-IN

The topic of mail-in (aka snail mail) sweepstakes is vast. This section could be a book unto itself. I do not plan to rewrite what many others have already written on the topic. There are many good books on the market today focusing on mail-in sweepstakes and a few of my favorite books are listed in the Recommended Reading section of this book. I will skim the topic to give you an overview.

Mail-in sweepstakes can be found in many places, including retail stores, magazines, newspapers, and online (some sweepstakes have entry forms you can download and print off at home). Mail-in sweepstakes in the United States are slowly getting harder to find as companies move towards online based promotions. This is a straight bottom line decision: it is far less expensive to run an online promotion than a mail-in promotion. The upside for sweepers is that there are fewer people entering mail-in sweepstakes, so the odds are getting better for those who do. The easiest way to find mail-in sweepstakes is to subscribe to one or more of the newsletters listed in this section.

There are many different ways a mail-in promotion can be run. Some ask for an Official Entry Form, a PPP (Plain Piece of Paper) or a postcard. You may be asked for a UPC (Universal Product Code) or a HDF (Hand Drawn Facsimile). There is a trend right now leaning away from UPCs and towards a short essay being submitted in lieu of a product purchase. The marketing and advertising idea behind requesting a product purchase or essay is to get the consumer involved with the product or services in a fun and creative way.

45

NOTE: If a sweepstakes has both a mail-in and Internet entry option, use the Internet option. Many companies treat mail-in entries like Internet entries by either coding them or opening the envelope and typing the information into the computer system. You are wasting time and money mailing in to these types of promotions. I always recommend entering via the Internet. It is only beneficial if the rules state one online entry and unlimited mail-in entries.

Like all sweepstakes, it's always important to read the rules so you know how many members of the household can enter, how often you can enter, the contest end date, how they would like the entry form sent in and if there is a No Purchase Entry option. This will determine your sweepstakes entry method(s). My personal favorites are one entry per person or one entry per household sweepstakes because: 1) everyone has an equal chance to win and 2) they take far less time to enter.

Staggering and Flooding

Staggering is the method of submitting entries "staggered" over the entire sweepstakes entry period. Flooding is the method of sending so many entries you have "flooded" the entry box, drawing drum or online database. This is also known as "mega entering".

Due to the drawing methods of mail-in promotions, it is a good idea to stagger your entries throughout the entire sweepstakes period. Due to the volume of mail most sweepstakes receive, it is impossible to put all the envelopes into the drawing drum and select the winner(s). Most judging agencies use one of the following methods:

1. Select a few entries from each mailbag and put those in the drum.
2. Select one mailbag and put those in the drum.
3. Put an entry code, similar to the online entries, on the envelope.
4. Open the envelope and enter your data into a computerized database for that sweepstakes.

Mailing in entries over the entire sweepstakes period increases the chances your entry will be in the drawing drum if the draw is using the first or second method. It doesn't help with methods three and four—

but then again; it doesn't hurt either. (See section, *Increasing Your Chances*.)

When you "flood" a sweepstakes, you are basically trying to increase the odds of having the winning entry form. Try this. Take a dice and throw it. The dice has six sides and the "odds" of you throwing a "one" is one in six. You may however throw the dice one hundred times and never have the "one" land face up. Each time you throw the dice the odds are still one in six. Now take a quarter or dime and throw it. You win if the coin lands face-up. The odds of this happening are one in two. Try throwing a coin a number of times and count how many times you get the face-up. You could throw the coin one hundred times and never have it land face-up, on the other hand it could land face-up each and every time. The odds are still one in two.

By flooding a sweepstakes you are increasing your chances of winning. That is a reality. However, even if you manage to have enough entries in the sweepstakes to be working with one-in-two odds, you may still not win.

Some people "flood" a sweepstakes and then get really upset when they don't win. They figure the judges are cheating or that they are blacklisted. If it is a nationally run sweepstakes, the more likely reality is that they just didn't get picked. On some of the local and in-store draw sweepstakes, they could be right, in which case you can increase your odds of winning by putting in fewer entries!

Extract from Winning Ways by Lynn Banks Goutbeck and Melanie Rockett. Used by permission of Proof Positive Productions Ltd. www.proofpositive.com.

Lingo

Abbreviations are generally associated with mail-in sweepstakes, but have sometimes been found in the rules of Internet sweepstakes. These are a few of the most common abbreviations you will come across while sweeping:

- NAZ/PH—Name Address Zipcode Phone Number
- NAZ and AGE—Name Address Zipcode Age
- OEB—Original Entry Blank
- SASE—Self Addressed Stamped Envelope
- UPC—Universal Product Code

TIP: If a sweepstakes asks for an essay with a specific word count (e.g. 500-word essay) type it out on your computer first, using a program like Microsoft Word, and using the WORD COUNT feature to get the precise word count. Then depending on the rules, you can either print it out and submit it or copy out by hand what you have just typed.

Postal Standards

The United States Postal Service (USPS) has set-out envelope and postcard addressing standards (along with other standards) that should be followed to ensure your mail-in entries are delivered properly. This is especially important if you choose to decorate, embellish or create your own envelopes. Size, weight and other factors may affect the amount of postage required or the mailability of your item.

You should visit the USPS website at: http://pe.usps.com/text/dmm300/dmm300_landing.htm and follow the addressing format, location guidelines and other requirements. Check back periodically as postal standards can and do change. You can also obtain the postal standards information at your local postal station or by mail.

TIP: Key search words to use on the USPS website include: address format; lettermail; non-mailable and envelopes.

Envelopes

I purposely put the USPS's postal standards before addressing this section on envelopes. Decorated, embellished and handmade envelopes

48

are very popular amongst mail-in sweepers. Most of the sweeping books I have read recommend mailing in envelopes "that stand out" to increase the odds of winning. The authors (and many fellow sweepers) feel they win more using these types of envelopes. I think the reason many sweepers believe they win with decorated, embellished and handmade envelopes is because they are using the Law of Attraction. (See chapter, *Attracting Luck*.) They are putting their winning thoughts and energies into and onto the envelope and sending it off into the Universe (via the USPS). This in turn sub-consciously attracts the person selecting the winner to that particular entry.

I have experimented using both types of envelopes. I have not found a difference in sending in plain envelopes vs. decorated ones. I currently send in plain envelopes. It is less time consuming to create and costs less money since I am not purchasing markers, stickers, glue, etc.

Lynn Goutbeck (co-author of *Winning Ways*) loved to decorate and embellish her envelopes. She even sent me a package once with examples of her envelopes because she was so excited about her cute designs. She saved money on envelopes by using all the ones that came in the mail with bills. Since they would be decorated, it didn't matter if they were plain or had writing and corporate logos on them. Lynn would purchase inexpensive used children's books and packs of used birthday cards, Christmas cards and postcards. She would cut the book pages and the cards to fit the envelope, glue pictures on the front and back, ensuring the flap would close properly, and put plain white labels where the return and mail-to addresses should go. She swore her designs were the source of her good fortune. I believed her.

I also met a woman (who asked to remain anonymous) who, in the last 12 years, has won 14 cars, over 125 trips and thousands of prizes. She sends in the plainest, simplest envelopes she can. She feels the judging agencies and sweepstakes management companies prefer to give away prizes to an average consumer rather than a "professional" sweeper. She said the colored and embellished envelopes are a dead give-away to the companies that it was sent in by a sweeper and her plain envelopes allow her to blend in with the average contestants. I cannot argue with her winning track record.

Try both methods and decide for yourself which one works better for you.

NOTE: If you choose to decorate or embellish your envelopes, ensure you adhere to USPS standards and do not draw, color, paint, glue or place stickers within the areas that are to remain clear. This will help ensure your entry is delivered properly. Also, keep all embellishments flat and do not use raised or puffy stickers, glue, paint etc. as they could catch in the postal machines, ruining your entry. This includes making sure that all of the edges of the envelope are smooth and straight. The last thing you want is to spend hours on a special envelope, only to have it be accidentally ripped open by a letter sorting machine.

TIP: Use a standard #10 business-sized envelope for your mail-in entries. Many companies I interviewed said if the envelope is too large, it will not fit into the drawing drum. The entry would then either be removed and placed into a smaller envelope or discarded altogether.

Harriet from Rockford, IL has allowed me to reprint her step-by-step directions for making your own envelopes.

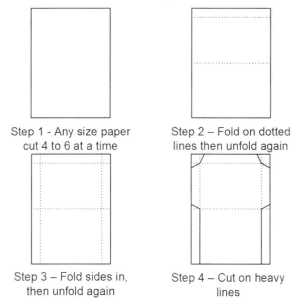

Step 1 - Any size paper
cut 4 to 6 at a time

Step 2 – Fold on dotted
lines then unfold again

Step 3 – Fold sides in,
then unfold again

Step 4 – Cut on heavy
lines

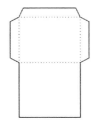

Step 5 – After cutting

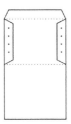

Step 6 – Fold in sides & put glue along dots and fold up bottom

Step 7 – Put finished envelope under a heavy book for a few minutes

Step 8 – When ready to use, put glue on flap and fold down. Use a heavy book for a few minutes to assure glue sticks

NOTE: If you choose to make your own envelopes, check the USPS website regarding postal standards to ensure your envelopes will be mailable.

Postcards

Many sweepstakes ask you to send in your entry on a postcard. I do not pay for postcards. I get my postcards free from postcard advertising displays found in various local shops and restaurants. I even grabbed a few every time I saw some in Europe on a trip we won, hoping some of the winning mojo would continue onto the next sweepstakes. (See chapter, *Attracting Luck.*)

TIP: Turn the postcard vertically and write the FROM information perpendicular to the TO information. I do this because a friend of mine was a postal employee and told me the machines send the card to whichever address they "read" first. If the FROM address is sideways it will not be read.

A standard postcard is 4¼ x 6. If a sweepstake asks for a 3 x 5 postcard, you can cut a regular unstamped postcard down and place it in an envelope. A 3 x 5 postcard is too small to mail according USPS mailing guidelines. The minimum is 3½ x 5. Often companies request a 3 x 5 postcard in error or misuse the term "postcard" when they mean an index card.

As long as the rules do not specifically state the required postcard's dimensions, another option is to use shaped postcards, although additional postage may apply. These are usually sold alongside regular postcards. They are a bit more expensive: however the card's surface area is generally much larger than a standard postcard and the varied sides could provide a better opportunity to be selected.

NOTE: Before sending shaped postcards, check with your local post office as the shaped postcards may require additional postage.

STORY: Harriet from Rockford, IL has been contesting and sweeping for over 60 years. In 1978 she wrote a book called The Winning Road. She wanted to share her love and knowledge of the hobby with others the same way I am now. Her philosophy and mine are alike. We both believe this hobby can change your life in exciting, fun and unexpected ways.

When my first husband was committed to a mental institution in 1953, I found myself on the 'road to despair'. To support myself and two young sons, I had to quickly find a job and adjust to an entirely new life style. Fortunately for us all I was picked up along the way by a new hobby, that of entering the various contests I saw in women's magazines.

By sheer coincidence (or was it fate?), I met a woman at a party who suggested that I subscribe to one of several contest publications currently on the market. I did and found that by expanding my creative efforts in skill contests, and by increasing my volume in sweepstakes, I was soon on the winning road.

In the next few years I won fun things such as radios, toys, phonographs, TV's, a backyard train that would carry three people, a trip to the baseball All-Star game, and a mink stole. And we won necessities, too, like a washer and dryer, two months supply of groceries, a power mower, and various cash prizes. But I think the real value of contesting was not so much in the prizes won, but rather in the intangibles. It gave my "fatherless" children something the other kids envied, channeled my own mental and physical energies to keep me out of mischief, and, more importantly, gave us all something to look forward to. We began to hate legal holidays because there were no mail deliveries!

I found the contest hobby like having an eccentric rich uncle who gives gifts sporadically but not always things wanted or needed. I won a diamond-tipped phonograph needle when I had no phonograph, an electric hedge trimmer when I had no hedge, and four dozen diapers when I had no baby. But I didn't care. I had the joy of winning and unneeded prizes could be bartered, sold, or given away.

In 1960, with the help of a local attorney and my company credit union, I was able to go to Las Vegas and get a divorce. Shortly thereafter I met my present husband on a blind date and married him the next year. Not only had my life changed, but the contest world had also. Instead of the emphasis being on skill contests, and only an occasional sweepstakes, it was the other way around. But no matter, I didn't NEED contests anymore. I still entered occasionally, winning proportionately, but other things had taken priority and I wouldn't have wanted it any other way.

1n 1977, however, my life changed again. My husband had a heart condition that worsened and resulted in his subsequent retirement. With a greatly reduced income and with children and grand children in need of a "rich uncle" I felt the urge to once again recharge my contest batteries.

For a long time I had noticed that people usually responded to my enthusiastic endorsement of contesting and would take me up on my offer to help them get started. And though I found great joy when one of my protégées won a big prize, it did take a lot of my time and energy to take them under my wing and get them started. So I decided to take a dream of mine and make it a reality. That dream was to write a book on contesting, a book that would share my experiences, my frustrations, and my exhilarations. More importantly, it would give step-by-step guide to the novice to get him started on the winning road. To do this I felt I needed more up-to-date credibility; that is, I needed to win a LOT of prizes, including at least one grand prize.

So I decided to once again move contesting to a priority position in my life. I searched out every skill and sweepstakes contest I could find. I subscribed to several contest publications, newspapers, and magazines, and read and absorbed numerous testimonials from big winners, and then I carefully developed my own winning system. And it worked! In 1978 I won 66 prizes, including a CB radio, tennis racket, football, soccer ball, clock radio, food processor, and various cash prizes, the largest $100. And then it happened. I won BIG! I won the Freshen-up Gum Sweepstakes grand prize, an all-expense paid trip to Hawaii for two plus $500 cash.

What follows is my dream book. I've left nothing out. It represents what I've learned in 25 years along the winning road. I've suffered long dry spells; once I spent five long months in the valley without a win, but I've also been to the mountain top with five prizes in a single day. Oh, occasionally I travel fast and get nowhere and win big when I have been walking, but over the long haul I win in direct proportion to the amount of horsepower devoted to the task.

There's a wide, beautiful, exciting road out there strewn with prizes to be picked up by steady, patient, persistent drivers. Come join me on my trip down the winning road. I'll show you the way…

Extract from *The Winning Road* and reprinted with permission from Harriet Brown.

Sweeping Supplies

Alaska N Cyber Gifts

www.alaskancybergifts.com/Sweepstake_Supplies.html

Joyce Gilliam first started her website to sell Alaskan made products; sadly, that didn't work out. In 2006 she decided to sell sweeping supplies and began at the 18th Annual National Sweepstakes Convention sharing a vendor table with Anita Moffet. She had so much fun she knew her decision had been a good one. Like me, she also enjoys combining her business with her hobby as it never feels like "work."

Joyce sells envelopes, stickers and address labels, index cards and papers. Her specialty is her stickers and labels as hers are geared to sweepstakes and holidays.

Every first order gets free index cards. If you order more than $50.00, you can also get your order shipped free and since you are ordering from Alaska, there is no state tax.

Alaska N Cyber Gifts
PO Box 210008
Anchorage, AK 99521

ANN-tics by Carol

https://home.comcast.net/~ann-tics/

Carol McLaughlin has been entering sweepstakes since 1968, and started her sweepstakes business in 2002 because of her love for arts and crafts, and to fill the void after losing her mother, Ann, in 2001. Carol and her mom did a lot of craft projects together and were always up to various antics so the name was a natural fit. Her signature ANN-tics envelopes and postcards have a computer graphic on the front to which she has added a cute or comical sweepstakes related saying. One could spend quite a bit of time going over and laughing at the different sayings. She now offers a full line of sweepstakes supplies, which include all kinds of envelopes and postcards such as: bubble print, fluorescent polka dot, shaving cream, printed paper (similar to wallpaper but no glue backing), 3 x 5 and other sized cards and papers for entries, and many items too numerous to list. She has a webpage that also includes a slideshow in order to view some of her supplies and gift baskets. The site often lists tidbits of information on sweepstaking news and events.

Carol also owns This N' That Sweepstakes Stuff newsletter.

ANN-tics by Carol
528 Princess Avenue
Croydon, PA 19021

Cheyenne Designs
www.cheyennedesigns.net

ShariAnne Fischer started selling her creations in 2001. She started making the envelopes for her own sweepstakes entries. Then ShariAnne began making them for her family. Members of her local club started buying from her and they encouraged her to get a vendor table at the 2002 national sweepstakes convention. Her specialty is hand painted envelopes with designs such as smooshed and webbed fantasy. She also sells; rainbow, gilded, and polished stones.

Cheyenne Designs
5660 E. Fox Street
Mesa, AZ 85205

CJ's Designs
cjenvelopes@yahoo.com

Carolyn Sayward started her business in 1999 after she suffered a stroke. She originally designed the envelopes for her husband, Al, to use for his sweepstakes. Al gave a few samples to his fellow club members and her business was born. Carolyn gets really excited when her customers tell her of their big wins using their envelopes. It is this type of response to the envelopes that keeps her going and as long as people like their envelopes, and win, they'll keep making them.

Carolyn specializes in computer generated graphic designs. They have every theme you can think of, including: Animals, Sports, People, Holidays, Trips and Automotive. Email Carolyn to request an order form.

CJ's Designer Envelopes
P.O. Box 463131
Mt. Clemens, MI 48046-3131

Econoprint Sweep Shop
www.sweepnshop.com

Frank Armstrong started the business in 1989, and Anita Moffatt bought it in 1995. Anita didn't become a sweeper until after attending her first national convention in 1997. Anita decided to retire in 2007 and sold the business to Amy Canganelli. After running a large manufacturing firm and teaching for many years, Amy began a family. Being blessed with twins didn't keep her busy enough so she decided to run her own business!

Econoprint offers a large selection of different colors, weights and sizes of envelopes their specialty being heavy weight colored envelopes: 60lb., 90lb. and 110lb. They also carry postcards and papers (slips) in various sizes and color. You can enter a monthly drawing for 250 free envelopes. No purchase necessary. See website for full rules.

Econoprint Sweep Shop
P.O. Box 2379
Silver Springs, FL 34489-2379

Elegant Envelopes
www.geocities.com/grannycmsc/index.html

Carol Colvin started her business in 2003. Her family is enthusiastic about recycling. One day she discovered a local paint store throwing away their wallpaper books. She wondered what she could do with the paper and discovered wallpaper envelopes online. So Carol got out her utility knife and started cutting. It was quite a chore until one day her son got out his electric saw and cut the backbone off the book.

When Carol began selling her envelopes on eBay she had never heard of sweeping, but she soon learned when people told her what sizes they wanted and she started making them. She has since become a sweeper!

In four years, her envelopes have kept over 4,000 pounds of paper out of the city dump. Any paper she has left over goes to a recycle center. She also makes postcards and Thank You notes.

Elegant Envelopes
280 Fish Haven Road
Lake Ozark, MO 65049

K.C. Supplies
www.kcsupplies.net

Karen Weix has been a sweeper for over 15 years. She started with a friend at a Rebate Club. A fellow member kept talking about all the trips she was winning and invited Karen and her friend to attend the next meeting. It was a year before they attended and couldn't figure out why they waited so long to start sweeping! Many years later she has won everything from fully paid vacations, to going to the Olympics, tickets to sport games, plays and concerts, as well as winning cash and cars!

Karen started K.C. Supplies at an Annual National Sweepstakes Convention. She reserved a vendor table alongside a friend and they began with a few supplies and some small raffles. Each year, as the convention grew so did K.C. Supplies. Customers now have access to a variety of envelopes, postcards, papers, stickers and other must-have sweeping supplies all year round by mail or online. Her sweeping supplies have helped bring luck and big wins to many of her customers, friends and sweeping buddies across the country.

She has been a member of the Illini Dream Team since she started sweepstaking, and currently is one of the board members.

K. C. Supplies
368 Forest Preserve Drive
Wood Dale, IL 60191

Print My 3x5s
www.printmy3x5s.com

Jennifer Day began her hand printing service and her sweepstaking hobby almost at the same time in 1997. She hand prints your information on 3 x 5 cards and paper along with 4 x 6 postcards. Her prices include the cost of the paper, cards and postcards along with shipping. She also has digital corporate logoed #10 envelopes.

Jenn has always had very clear and neat handwriting. Her service is invaluable to those with poor handwriting or who have problems with their hands, as many sweepstakes request hand printed information. She gives away 100 hand printed papers every month. Check her website for details.

Print My 3x5s
3324 Parker
Dearborn, MI 48124

Shape Postcards
www.shapepostcards.com

David and Terry Brown started the business in 2002 after they had tremendous success using shaped postcards in local sweepstakes. David passed away in 2004 and Terry decided to keep the business.

Available postcard shapes include: animals, food, cartoons, travel and cash. Terry has a 10 postcard Sample Pack for new customers and has a Specials page for those who wish to save a bit of money.

Shape Postcards
PMB 174
2657-G Annapolis Road
Hanover, MD 21076-1262

NOTE: All Shape Postcards take a 41¢ stamp for mailing. Some require an extra 12¢ stamp for a non-machineable surcharge. Check with your local post office for proper postage rates. (See section, Postal Standards.)

TIP: You can use the travel and cash postcards on your sweepstaking goal chart or vision board. (See chapter, Attracting Luck.)

Shelly's Handprinting Service
www.webspawner.com/users/handprinting/

Shelly G. has been a sweepstaker for over 15 years and began her handprinting service in 2005. Her neat handwriting made it a natural venture for her when she decided to start a home-based business.

Shelly hand prints your information on 3 x 5 cards and papers along with envelopes. She also sells decorated envelopes utilizing her extensive collection of art rubber stamps.

Contact Shelly by email: shells1234@webtv.net or by mail:

Shelly's Handprinting
P.O. Box 9403
Cincinnati, OH 45209

Sweepstake Supplies
www.sweepstakesupplies.com

Cindy Kuptz started Sweepstake Supplies in 2002. As a sweeper, she found herself using a substantial amount of postcards and envelopes. She wanted to pass on the savings of the unusual or eye-catching designs she found to fellow sweepers.

Cindy carries a wonderful assortment of bright, eye catching envelopes, postcards, and 3½ x 5 cards and papers. All of her envelopes are manufactured by leading envelope companies. Since her prices are already below retail she only offers discounts on large quantity orders.

Sign-up for her monthly newsletter: The Supply Line.

Sweepstake Supplies
PO Box 342
Novi, MI 48375

Victoria's Handprinting Service
oldestbrat@peoplepc.com

Victoria Barber started handprinting in 2002 for family members that need a bit of extra help with their entries. She decided to turn her helping hands into a business in 2004.

Victoria offers handprinting on 3 x 5 and 3 ½ x 5 cards and papers, SASE #10, bright and pastel envelopes. She makes fabric and scrapbook paper envelopes that she sells at each national convention. If she hasn't sold out, she makes her inventory available to her handprinting customers. She also places a few extra sweepstaking goodies into each order such as handmade envelopes or postcards.

Victoria sends out an email newsletter every three month with specials on prices for that quarter. The quickest way to order is to send Victoria an email.

Victoria's Handprinting Service
3840 W. Northern Avenue
Camp Verde, AZ 86322

TIP: If you purchase inexpensive envelopes be aware that the glue on the seal doesn't always meet the envelope correctly. It can overlap the opening and stick to your 3 x 5 entry. Therefore, when putting your entry into the envelope ensure the addressed side is facing away so the blank side is facing the seal. Then if the glue leaks onto your entry, it will not rip off your information when opened.

Craig and I had a GREAT win via mail. It was a promotion being held by a very popular fabric softener company. They had sent a sample to our house to try a new scent. Along with the sample was a mail-in entry to win a washer and dryer or a few other prizes. It was a one entry per household sweepstakes.

One day our mailperson came to the door with a registered letter. I had won first prize: a $2,000 Roots (www.roots.com) gift certificate! I needed a new winter coat, and had never owned a leather jacket… and besides, a girl can never have too many purses!

It was mid-December when we won. I knew if I mailed the affidavit and release forms back in the enclosed envelope they could get lost or delayed in the Christmas mail. I chose to spend the money and couriered the forms back. That was a wise decision for two reasons: 1) I knew that it got there, and 2) they were able to send my gift certificates back to me right away. My husband and I were able to buy far more than we normally would have because of the great Boxing Day sales.

NOTE: Boxing Day in Canada is December 26th and is our biggest retail sales day of the year, similar to Black Friday in the United States.

What I found ironic was that on the entry form they had asked my opinion on the new scent and I told them the truth. I did not like it, I

61

thought it smelled like bubble gum and I would not buy this particular scent, ever! I still won and I do buy their original scent.

STORY: Over 50 years ago, sweeping was considered a "women's" hobby. (See chapter, Joining a Sweeping Club.) As the hobby evolved into allowing online and cellphone entries, more and more men have become sweepers. Here is the story of a <u>winner</u> we can all be inspired by.

෨෨

Polli—Rockville, MD

Imagine my surprise when I received a package from Johnny Mathis. My sixteen year old mind was whirling! What could it be? It was an autographed record album of "A Certain Smile"! I had entered a contest using a photograph of me smiling. I guess it was a winner. I was so thrilled! I was the talk of my high school the following day. That record album was the beginning of what was to become my much-loved hobby.

That first win was in 1959. There have been many twists and turns to my life from that point on and still I forged on with my sweepstaking. I have gone places that were only dreams and experienced them with my loving husband, Stanley and two daughters, Lisa Beth and Melynda Debra.

We traveled to China in 2000 and saw the antiquities of the ancients, to California several times to see how wine is made and how dreams come true within the film industry. We stayed at the fabled Hotel Del Coronado where I saw my first ghost! What a historical place that is!

I won a Halloween trip to Disney World for our daughter and her friend. She was treated like the princess she is and had a wonderful time. She regales her three young sons with stories from that trip.

Last year we saw the sun set in Aruba. How breathtaking and serene. We have heard exquisite symphonies at Wolf Trap in Virginia and eaten dinner under the stars many times. In 1986, we spent a New Year's Weekend at the Hyatt Regency in Bethesda, Maryland which included all the amenities (dancing, dining, hats and noise makers) and pampering one could ask for.

I have won four trips to Los Angeles, California which is always a thrill as our older daughter, Allie Raye (Lisa Beth), is a hard-working actress in that great fun-loving city! We have all stayed at the magnificent Pan Pacific Hotel and took up an entire floor for our Penthouse one year. How great was that! These are memories that our children will take with them forever; all thanks to sweepstaking.

One of my acts of "giving back" was in 1994 when I won a Thanksgiving Dinner for twenty people sponsored by Safeway and Nabisco Biscuit Company. I donated the entire Dinner to Second Genesis, which is a Drug and Alcohol Rehabilitation Center. The way I felt when everyone thanked me was worth everything to me.

In 1991 I shared a $2500 shopping spree with one of our daughters. She had a terrific time tearing clothes and shoes off the racks of the "Woodies" Department Store! We still giggle about it today! In 1997, I won for this same lucky daughter and her new husband, a Honeymoon Cruise on Norwegian Cruise Line to the Southern Caribbean. They had a wonderful time and were treated like VIPs!!

In 1995, my family of four went on an unforgettable trip to San Diego, California. This trip included all the amenities: travel, rental car, meals, tickets to the San Diego Zoo and a gorgeous harbor cruise. It was sponsored by WASH-FM and Pillsbury. The pictures we took show our joy!

Gillette and Kmart sponsored a $25,000 Putting Challenge in Greensboro, North Carolina. I won a place for my husband! He did beautifully and missed the BIG ONE by a quarter of an inch! He still enjoyed a check for $500.00 from Kmart. Gillette paid for everything for us: our travel expenses, food, rental car, cash… everything. Reporters were scattered around the golf course taking pictures and chatting up the contestants during the entire game! How exciting was that! Gillette sent us a video of the whole afternoon of fun and frolic. It was an unforgettable experience for my husband and I.

Our local television station, WMAL, sponsored a Disney Contest Odyssey Cruise on the Potomac River. My husband and I were treated to a day of WINS, Disney "stuff", Radio contests, more wins, more "stuff"! The day on the Potomac was beautiful, warm and sunny. A lovely time for all.

When I was a child in Altoona, Pennsylvania, we slept under Hudson Bay Blankets because of the bitter cold winters. Imagine how thrilled I was when I won a Hudson Bay Blanket in 1999. I shared both the blanket and the story with my family. Also in 1999, I won a 48" Television from Best Buy in a Kimberly-Clark Sweeps. What enjoyment that was!

I was fortunate to win, two years in a row, the "Come Meet the Stars" Sweepstakes! This sweepstakes benefited the Children's Cancer Foundation. It was held at the Marriott Hunt Valley Inn, in Maryland.

One year I was lucky to win a dance with one of the Soap Stars and he sang just to me!! All my friends were green with envy!! Another year, my husband bid for a picture of one of the Soap Stars and won it!! I still have that picture hanging in my study.

In 2000 I also won a beautiful purple Baby Jogger that I gifted to our new grandson, Asher Hillel! My daughter's children still play with that jogger and enjoy flying down the street with Melynda on roller blades. .

In 1995-1996, I went through chemotherapy and radiation for cancer. The fact that I could retreat into my study, pull out my sweepstakes supplies and concentrate on which sweeps to enter, was a welcome respite. I feel strongly that being able to sweepstake aided in my recovery.

Since this story is about me and my sweepstaking career, I will say that my hobby is one I hold close to my heart. It has been my "Peter Pan"— taking me among the stars. I have met some wonderful warm individuals along this path and plan to continue to do so. Even though I feel the game has changed, the "thrill of the game" is still there for me.

Thank you Johnny Mathis for starting me on my Road to WINS.

༄༅

Newsletters

NOTE: All the newsletters listed are paid subscription publications. Please check with each publication for current subscription rates.

Best Publications
www.bestsweepstakes.com

Nick Taylor has been a sweeper for more than 25 years. He is very entrepreneurial and was looking for a new business idea. Like myself, Nick combined his love of the hobby and his business savvy and created Best Publications 15 years ago. Best Publications prints three newsletters: Best Sweepstakes Newsletter, Best Extra and Best Weekly. He launched a companion website eight years ago. Subscribers have access to new online sweepstakes links, a chat room, forum and regional sweepstakes. Nick also has a monthly online sweepstakes. Check site for full details and rules.

Best Publications
PO Box 421163
Plymouth, MN 55442

Sweeper Times
http://thesweepertimes.com

Allen Sayward (aka Captain Jack) came to the hobby naturally as his parents are Al and Carolyn Sayward (CJ's Designs). He wanted to create a fun sweeping newsletter focusing on the details within the official rules. The first issue was printed in mid-2006.

Readers can participate in subscriber-only sweepstakes by submitting sweepstakes they feel their fellow sweepers would enjoy entering. If selected, the submitter has two free issues of Sweeper Times added to their subscription. If not, they get an entry into the monthly draw. They also run a word scramble contest for their subscribers giving away sweepstakes related items as prizes.

Submit questions to Captain Jack and read his answer in a future issue. They also print Sweepstaker Horoscopes giving the reader a tongue-in-cheek glimpse into their winning future. Sweeper Times is only available by mail and is published every two weeks.

Sweeper Times
PO Box 4264
Camp Verde, AZ 86322

SweepSheet®

www.sweepsheet.com

Sandy Gulliver is a sweepstaker and loves entering. She took the best from each of the newsletters she subscribed to and launched SweepSheet® in 1989 at the 1st Annual National Sweepstakes Convention. In 2008 Sandy Retired. Patti and Kurt Osterheld became the new owners with Patti as Editor.

Sweepsheet is a bi-weekly newsletter available either by mail or as an online downloadable PDF. Sections include: Profile of a Fanatical Sweepstaker, Sweepstakes, Contests, In-Stores and Winners.

Subscribers also get access to the Member's Only section of the website. Exclusive features include: Hot Flashes, Conversation Corner and an Index of all the sweepstakes printed in every issue.

SweepSheet®
105 Town Line Road
PBM 329
Vernon Hills, IL 60061

This N' That Sweepstakes Stuff

http://home.comcast.net/~tnte-mail/

Deb Houin created This N' That in 1998. In 2007 when Deb decided she needed to spend more time running her family's farm, Carol McLaughlin, owner of ANN-tics by Carol Sweepstakes Supplies, offered to take it over.

Unlike other publications that list sweepstakes, This N' That is a collection of stories, tips, monthly drawings and email, pen pal, birthday clubs. It is a fun newsletter for those that do not have a sweepstakes club near them and would like to be part of the sweeping community. For further information, via mail, send a SASE to the address below.

This N' That Sweepstakes Stuff
528 Princess Avenue
Croydon, PA 19021

ONLINE

My favorite way to enter sweepstakes is via the Internet. It's fast, free, and there are more and more promotions online every day. The downside is, since it is so quick and easy to enter, more and more people have picked up Internet sweeping as a hobby. This means more competition, which affects the odds of winning.

The main focus of this book is on the fast growing method of Internet sweeping. In the following chapters, I will discuss the many ways you can use the Internet to enhance your hobby, including websites that feature portals to newsletters, forums where you can meet like-minded people online, sites that host online promotions, and methods of protecting yourself from identity theft, hackers and con artists plus how to protect your computer against viruses and spam.

NOTE: Do not fear monitored websites, forums or chat rooms. The monitoring is not designed to be "Big Brother," rather it is to prevent any type of online abuse and keeps the site safe and clean for its participants.

> *"You can't lose helping others win."*
> *Anonymous*

Websites

There are many U.S. websites and blogs that either post sweepstakes online directly or offer a link to a newsletter subscription.
NOTE: ✉ = free e-newsletter offered on website.

About Contests ✉
Website: http://contests.about.com
Forum: http://contests.about.com/mpboards.htm

Sandra Grauschopf took over the Contests and Sweepstakes section of About.com in 2007 after long-time sweepstakes experts Tom Stamatson and his wife Ingrid retired. Entering sweepstakes is Sandra's passion, and she has been studying the hobby for the past five years. She loves being able to share her knowledge and help others win, as well as the camaraderie the sweepstaking community offers.

There are quite a few sweepstakes resources available on the About Contests website, the How-To articles being my favorite. Click on STAY-UP-TO-DATE to sign-up for her free e-newsletter or to receive her online sweepstakes courses (via email).

TIP: Ensure whenever you sign up for emails coming from a major website you set your spam filters to accept emails from that organization (e.g. contests.about.com).

CashNet Sweepstakes
Website: www.cashnetsweeps.com
Forum: www.sweeps247.com

In 1997, Amanda Adams, launched CashNet as a website focused on freebies. Her hobby turned into a full-time venture when her family grew and she wanted to be a stay-at-home mom. Amanda's interests moved to running a sweepstakes directory as she always enjoyed winning prizes and discovered a lack of online sweepstakes resources.

Members of CashNet are given access to SweepsTracker, a free sweepstakes entry tracking program and a personal wins page, where each member can post a list of their wins to share with family and friends. CashNet also has an active community forum where sweepers can find information, answers, advice and friends.

TIP: Keep a small notebook by your computer to write notes, codes and UPCs for current sweepstakes and future reference.

Contest Blogger
Forum: www.contestblogger.com
Blog: www.contestblogger.com/blog

Phil Van Treuren started Contest Blogger mid-2007. Contest Blogger was the first blog dedicating to showcasing blog contests. Many blogs were running contests but until Contest Blogger, there wasn't a publicity vehicle for them.

The forum is an online gathering place for sweepstakers featuring sections such as: Cash Prize Online Contests, Blog Contests and Writing Project Contests.

You must be a member to post in the forum. Membership is free. Subscribe to his blog's RSS (Really Simple Syndication) feed as Phil regularly posts about cool online contests, moneymaking tips and other fun stuff.

NOTE: Blogger-based sweepstakes sites are being created at a rapid rate due to the ease of setting up a blog versus a website. Check the Blogroll on my blog, www.fromthe.contestqueen.com, to find sweepstakes blog links.

Contest Girl ✉

Website: www.contestgirl.com

Contest Girl is owned and operated by Linda Horricks. She started her website in 2006 and it lists sweepstakes and contests for the U.S., Canada and even some internationally. She stumbled across online sweepstaking after her sister won a cruise. When Linda began having success, her friends and family began to ask her for help. After emailing interesting sweepstakes to all these different people many times over, she saw a need for a better way of telling people about sweepstakes and for screening them to avoid the ones that were "scammy" or "spammy". Her husband, Martin, manages the technical aspects of the site, while Linda creates the content.

It is organized by location and entry frequency. There is even a feature called; My Contests, which allows you to select and organize the sweepstakes you are most interested in, saving you valuable entry time. There is also a Free Stuff section for those that like freebies.

Contest Guru ✉

Website: www.contestguru.com
Blog: http://contestguru.com/contestnews/

Contest Guru is owned by Melanie Rockett. You may recognize her as the co-author (with Lynn Goutbeck) of "Winning Ways," a top-selling contesting book in the early 90's. Melanie has a new book called "Contest Guru's Guide to Winning Sweepstakes." It is available for a small fee on her website as a downloadable e-book, www.proofpositive.com/contestnews.htm.

In addition to being a sweepstakes enthusiast, Melanie is also interested in skill-based contests. Seven years ago she launched www.proofpositive.com as a way of helping and mentoring other freelance writers and photographers. She encourages freelancers to enter skill-based contests as a self-promotion strategy. The contesting portion of her site became so popular that she spun it off to a new website www.contestguru.com. Contest Guru has hundreds of skill-based contests for writers, poets, photographers, song writers and cooks as well as contests that focus on short essays, slogans and jingles.

You can sign-up for her newsletter which is free of charge and which is sent out on a sporadic (when there is news) basis.

ContestHound.com ✉

Website: www.contesthound.com
Newsletter: www.contesthound.ca/newsletter.php3?siteID=edge

Bob Gunther started ContestHound.com in 1999 after his first daughter was born and he decided to be a stay-at-home dad. Now working alongside his wife, the site is easy to navigate allowing you to search on sweepstakes based on time frames such as Daily, Weekly, One Time Only, etc. There is a free membership available, allowing you to login and keep track of your contests in My Contests.

You can also sign-up for the free e-newsletter that comes out approximately twice a week. The newsletter always features a story about their kids and their life as stay-at-home, work-at-home parents. Very funny!

Contests Sweepstakes 4 Free ✉

Website: www.contests-sweepstakes-4free.com
Blog: www.contest-canada.blogspot.com

Bernard Tiraloche launched Contests Sweepstakes 4 Free featuring sweepstakes open to both Americans and Canadians. The site features regionalized sweepstakes listings so it is easier for you to find a promotion open to you. They have also incorporated a SNAP reader into the site so you can preview a page without clicking on it.

Bernard also runs the website www.usa1sweepstakes.com.

Gimme Sweeps
Website: www.gimmesweeps.com

After Ingrid Stamatson retired from running the sweepstakes site at About.com, she began her own site, Gimme Sweeps! The site features a front page blog with newly-found sweepstakes and freebies, plus all links to the Prize pages, Ending Soon, Daily Entry pages are easily accessed right from that front page.

The new Daily Entry section eliminates the need for bookmarks or external programs to keep track of your dailies, as they are arranged by month as they expire, and all you do is follow the pages for the coming months.

The site is free to use, no membership is required, but donations are appreciated to defray the costs of running the website.

Hypersweep ✉
Website: www.hypersweep.com
Forum: www.hypersweep.com/forums

Scott Bourgeois started Hypersweep in 1999 at a time when there were relatively few sweepstakes focused websites. All visitors can browse their real-time database of online sweepstakes at no cost. Registered members have access to more robust features such as the ability to add sweepstakes to the site, earn entries into members-only drawings, and even earn free membership. The site automatically keeps track of your entries, and remembers the last time each sweepstakes was entered. Other advanced features include a personalized favorites list, a built-in form fill assistant, and even an automated entry system. Members can also interact through an instant message system. To help members avoid scams, all promotions are archived so you can confirm a winning notification is legitimate. Anyone can read the forum, but you must be a member to post messages. Members can also join a private mailing list with direct links to all new sweepstakes posted on the site the previous day.

Non-members who have purchased this book can also sign-up for the Hypersweep private mailing list by using the URL: www.hypersweep.com/CQ and the password CQFREE.

Online-Sweepstakes.com

Website: www.online-sweepstakes.com
Forum: forums.online-sweepstakes.com

Online-Sweepstakes.com (OLS) was launched by Brent Riley in December of 1997. With a lifelong interest in computers and programming and a desire to learn how to design and program web sites, Brent decided to create a web site specializing in the listing of sweepstakes and contests for sweepers. An occasional sweeper himself, Brent set out with the goal of designing a sweepstakes site that could help improve sweepers' chances of winning as much as possible.

Over the last 10 years, OLS has become the largest sweepstakes directory and community of sweepers on the Internet. Featuring a fast, simple and easy to use web site, a number of advanced and unique features that make finding, entering and winning sweepstakes easier and less time-consuming, and a very active message board of experienced and helpful sweepers, OLS is a community-centric sweepstakes site that helps its members and visitors win millions of dollars in cash and prizes every year.

OLS offers sweepers two levels of membership, Free and Premium. The Free membership gives you access to thousands of sweepstakes and most of the various features of the web site. The Premium membership costs $30 per year and gives you access to a few thousand additional sweepstakes that are generally more difficult to find and less popular than those available with Free membership. Premium membership also includes an ad-free web site, a few more advanced features that help you organize and track your entries and a unique tool called Shazam! that really helps speed up your online entries.

Power Sweepstaking

Website: www.powersweepstaking.com

Ron Miller created Power Sweepstaking for you to be able to enter more sweepstakes faster and more efficiently. He felt scanning various online sites, groups and forums for promotions was too time consuming. Like myself, Ron has an extensive marketing background and he leveraged his knowledge to create a system to enter more sweepstakes, faster. Power Sweepstaking has twenty-two blogs covering such topics as: Winner's Lists, Sweepstakes Press Releases and Sweepstakes Answers. A daily email is sent out with links with those three blog updates. You can also receive additional information via RSS feed.

You can become a basic member of Power Sweepstaking for free. To take advantage of all the features, you can purchase an annual subscription.

Sweepstakes Advantage ✉

Website: www.sweepsadvantage.com
Forum: www.sweepsadvantage.com/smf

Ken and Diane Carlos started in 1997 as a way to make ends meet. At that time, Diane was a stay-at-home mom looking for a way to supplement the family income. Entering sweepstakes looked like a good way to spend time while seeking employment. When the wins actually started showing up, they got the idea to start a sweepstakes website of their own. It felt good to create and offer something they believed in and offer to people at no cost. It was the perfect fit and has since become one of their greatest achievements in life.

Membership is free. Members are eligible to enter exclusive "SA Members Only Sweepstakes." There are also many useful online tools for members such as: Sweepscheck, My Sweepstakes, sweepstakes reminders, sweepstakes notes and expired sweepstakes archive to look up winner's list information.

There is also another unique tool called Prize Wish, www.prizewish.com, allowing one to search the web and possibly win a prize!

There is a daily and a weekly free e-newsletter available to members. They include: summaries of the latest sweepstake news, the top sweepstakes, insider tips plus freebies and coupons.

Sweepstakes Edge

Website: www.sweepstakesedge.com

Lisa LaFreniere started the website in 2000 as a way to share her love of sweeping with others. Originally known as Complete Sweeps, it was recreated as Sweepstakes Edge in 2007. Members enjoy access to the sweepstakes listing which is updated daily with both online and mail-in promotions. Members can comment on listings, rate them or save them to their own folder for future reference and entering. There is also a forum for members to chat about sweepstakes.

Membership was originally free, but to cover the costs of running an Internet presence three membership levels were introduced: Regular, Snail Mail and Lifetime. In addition to traditional memberships they have 25 Ambassador roles with free membership in exchange for assisting to maintain and improve the website. Memberships are limited to a total of 575. When openings are available the subscribe feature is online, once filled it's removed.

SweepsGoat ✉

Website: www.sweepsgoat.com
Blog: http://blog.sweepsgoat.com

Billy and Angela Mabray started SweepsGoat mid-2007 because they wanted to create a truly community-based sweepstakes website—one where anyone could add and vote for sweepstakes. Everyone can see all listed sweepstakes.

They offer a daily e-newsletter that lists newly added sweepstakes, either as soon as they're added or after they receive sufficient votes to reach the "Top Sweeps" page. They also offer RSS feeds and a Twitter feed for members who prefer more immediate notification. Their blog offers sweepstakes stories and a Friday round-up of the week's top-ranked sweeps.

A free membership is required to add sweepstakes, comment, or vote.

NOTE: Twitter is a social networking website where you can meet friends, family and colleagues online. http://twitter.com/

Sweepstakes Today ✉

Website: www.sweepstakestoday.com
Forum: www.sweepstakestoday.com/cs/forums/

Craig McDaniel picked up sweeping as a hobby after he underwent major surgery and had to give up a few of his favorite activities. He started entering online in 1999 after running a search for "sweepstakes" in a search engine. Craig (aka Mr. Sweepy) started Sweepstakes Today in 2004 after winning several major sweepstakes.

Sweepstakes are sorted into various categories including: Featured Sweepstakes, New Sweepstakes and Sponsor's Special Sweeps. You can also save your favorites on My Lucky List. There is a section for freebies and coupons too.

Membership is free, giving you access to the website, the forum and a monthly e-newsletter is sent to all members.

Google, MSN and Yahoo

Another online resource for finding sweepstakes are the online groups on Google (http://groups.google.com), MSN (http://groups.msn.com) and Yahoo (http://groups.yahoo.com). If you wish to search out a group or one of these websites, enter the keyword "sweepstakes" in the search bar.

NOTE: You must be a member of Google, MSN or Yahoo to join any of their groups, but membership to each of these sites is free.

SuperSweepstakes
Group: http://groups.yahoo.com/group/SuperSweepstakes/

Charmaine B. started SuperSweepstakes in 2002 and wanted to share her love of sweepstaking with others. 400 to 600 new sweepstakes are added by members each month. She also does specialized searches for prizes that her members most want to win and seeks out local sweeps for the regions her members live in.

To encourage group participation and to discourage "lurking," active posters on SuperSweepstakes get invited to her private group that features mail-in and larger-value prize sweepstakes. Charmaine also holds monthly prize drawings for stamps, envelopes for the active posters, as well as, random drawings for the whole group. She feels it adds some extra fun to her group. The group is currently open to U.S. and Canadian Members.

Charmaine also owns other groups TotallyFreeFreebies, ReferralSweepstakeBuddies and Instant Winners which are only open to SuperSweepstake members.

TIP: If there is an option, receive the group messages in digest form. They can be scanned through quite quickly. Also, potentially receiving hundreds of emails daily from "strangers" can be quite overwhelming. If you do choose to receive the groups in individual emails, set your email client up to move email from the group into a separate folder so it is automatically segregated from your personal and business correspondence.

NOTE: Many inactive groups are left on these sites. Read the message board to ensure the group has had recent postings and is active before joining.

STORY: Through writing this book I met many women like Carol (owner of ANN-tics). It never ceases to amaze me how this hobby can touch all aspects of one's life in such a positive way.

ℰ◌ℛ

Carol—Croydon, PA

The earliest I can remember entering sweepstakes was when I was a teen around 1968. My sister and I had entered a radio contest where we had to hand print the words "Kissin' Cousins" as many times as we could on a U. S. Post Card. The prize was a set of movie tickets to see Elvis Presley's new movie Kissin' Cousins and a record album with the music from the movie. My sister had the tiniest printing I ever saw and won the prize. We gathered a group of our friends and all walked the 3 miles from Pennsylvania over to Trenton, New Jersey to see the movie and shop for the afternoon.

I casually entered since then from entry forms I found in magazines, cereal boxes and store drop boxes. In 1977 when I was off on maternity leave with my first child, I began entering pretty regularly and one day saw a stamp in the Publishers Clearing House mailing to order a subscription to Contest Newsletter. I ordered it and was hooked after that!!

I don't remember where I found the rest of the newsletters that I started subscribing to, but it quickly went up to six, if not more, that I was receiving at a time. In those days they were all mail-ins and I entered a lot. I believe my very first win as an "addicted sweeper" was an autographed picture of Roger Staubach, then quarterback for the Dallas Cowboys, thanks to Contest Newsletter. Although many of the original newsletters have had gone by the wayside, either ceasing publication completely or merging with other newsletters, I am always to this day on the prowl for new and exciting newsletters and books on sweeping.

In the beginning I did not keep win notices, but I do have four 3-ring binders with the earliest win notice going back to 1978. I did get sloppy at times over the years and did not save all of my win notices so some of them are missing.

I had been hand decorating my envelopes for my own use by using colored markers and stickers. Then around 2002 I started making new designs on the computer. In 2004 I joined my very first sweeping club. I would take my decorated envelopes to the meetings and use them in the envelope exchange. Some of my friends wanted to buy them and that is how my business got started, on a limited basis.

My mom passed away in 2001 and starting this business was my way to fill the void and also to remember her. You see, my mom and I had always made handmade crafts together. We would sell them around the holidays at the local craft fairs. She always looked forward to the Christmas holidays and going to these events whether we sold items or not, just went to see what we could buy. I liked to go to keep her company, plus to sell my own handmade crafts. I appropriately named my sweeping business ANN-tics, a combination of the two words "ANN" (since that was my mother's name) and "antics" (for the fun that we always had together). The hummingbird in my logo was my mom's favorite bird/symbol. Her house and clothes were often decorated with them. When I would visit my parents at their summer place in the mountains, I would often sneak off to the store for shopping and before I left to return home would secretly place something that had a hummingbird somewhere in her home or around the yard. So I guess I could say I started the business to honor the good times I had with my mom.

I know she has become part of my business because every time I go to a convention or meeting of new friends I see something with butterflies on it. This was the first "sign" I saw while standing at her gravesite on a very cold Pennsylvanian November day. I always feel she is sharing in this hobby with me and just knowing this has helped me dig up the courage to travel to places to meet fellow sweepers that I never would have dreamed of. Through this inspiration and from the great sweepers I have met over the past three years, one being the author of this book, I have actually taken over the planning of and bringing to a reality a mini sweepstakes convention that will be attended by many coming from almost every state east of the Mississippi River, along with others from more western states and Canada. It's very exciting because many attendees have never had the opportunity to attend such an event.

I would like to close with how this hobby has changed my life in wonderful ways I never could have imagined.

80&03

TEXT MESSAGING

TXT (Text Messaging) or SMS (Short Message Service) on your cell phone is the newest form of sweeping. If you have not begun entering via your cell phone, you should start. Relatively few people enter these sweepstakes (compared to other methods of entering sweepstakes), so your odds of winning are very good. My husband and I have won many prizes from sweepstakes we entered on our cell phones.

There are two types of text sweepstakes: ones that are only entered via your cellphone, and ones that have an text entry component to them.

Always read the rules of every sweepstakes to see what the different entry methods are. If text messaging is an option, use it—if the only method of entry is via your cell phone, the odds of winning are the best of all the sweepstakes entry methods at this time, and if it is a component of a sweepstakes, it will usually garner you extra entries into the sweepstakes.

You will be asked to text a specific word, or phrase, to a word representing the company (PIZZA = 74992) or a short code. A fictitious example would be *text WIN to short code 123456.*

There are two basic keypad types: telephone style or keyboard style. Typically the telephone style is found on a cell phone and keyboard style is found on a Personal Digital Assistant (PDA) such as a RIM BlackBerry® or Palm Treo®. This is important, because if your are only given a word as the short code and you have a PDA, you will have to know what the letters transpose to, as the numbering and lettering will not match on the keyboard.

Many people do not have a messaging package with their wireless provider and are afraid to enter because each message could cost 15¢, 25¢, 50¢ or more. Yet, those same people will mail off dozens of entries into a promotion at 41¢ or more per letter, not including the cost of the envelope! Call your cell phone/wireless service provider and sign-up for a text messaging package today. (I currently pay $20.00 per month for 2500 messages, plus voicemail, call display and call waiting—a bargain when you consider what some sweepers spend on postage.)

*NOTE: If you see the words **premium message**, enter cautiously. These text sweepstakes cost anywhere from $1 to $5 and the fee will not be absorbed by your text messaging package today. You will be charged the premium message fee each and every time you enter.*

Since each cell phone is different, I suggest you read the manual for specific instructions on how to use your phone's messaging service. Here is a link for SMS short forms to help you get started, www.techdictionary.com/chatsms.html.

My husband, Craig, won our first prize from a text messaging contest. He won an "In The Action" game package consisting of two In The Action Seats to a specified Toronto Jays game, the opportunity to watch the team warm up, a "Behind The Scenes" tour of Rogers Centre, an official Jays jersey which he got autographed by three players, a golf shirt, two baseball hats and a Super Sports Pack twelve month subscription from Rogers Cable.

My father-in-law, is a HUGE baseball fan and flew in from British Columbia to join Craig at the practice and game. This so impressed the Jays' marketing staff they also gave my father-in-law an official Jays jersey (increasing the value of the win).

TIP: It never hurts to ask. It was at my request they threw in the extra jersey. It is up to the discretion of the sweepstakes sponsor to change or alter the prize.

STORY: I met Rick at one of my Canadian book signings. He told me he had used up all of his luck when he married his lovely wife. I told him it just confirmed he was lucky and to let me know when he won his first grand prize. It only took him six months to win a "big one" and although he is a member of my sweepstakes club, he still sent me an email letting me know about his win.

೩೧೪

Rick—Pickering, ON

I am fairly new to sweeping and I had been trying all of the different types of sweepstakes I came across. I thought I would try the text message sweepstakes and I stopped by my cellular provider to get a basic text message plan. Armed with 100 text messages per month I started to enter sweepstakes with my cell phone. After the first month of entries, the $85 text message bill and shocked comments from my wife confirmed that I needed the unlimited text message plan.

After upgrading my account, my friend Craig told me about a Molson's sweepstakes to "Win the Twins." I started to send the text message faithfully every day until the end of the sweepstakes. One day I checked a voice mail message and was stunned when the voice suggested that I was a grand prize winner. All I needed to do was contact them before a specific date. They administered the skill testing question and confirmed that I did indeed win the grand prize. I had won the "Twins": two brand new Harley Davidson motorcycles!

This was my first large grand prize win. I was surprised but there they were, two shiny new "Hogs." Needless to say, my wife no longer has any issue with my text message bill.

೩೧೪

"I'm a great believer in luck,
and I find the harder I work
the more I have of it."
Thomas Jefferson

ENTERING ONLINE

Entering online, or via the Internet, is becoming the most common way to enter sweepstakes. In the 1950s, judged contests were the most common type of promotions; to reduce administration costs, companies gradually shifted to sponsoring mail-in sweepstakes. Technology has moved forward over the past several decades, and personal computers have now become as common as television in most households. Again, due to administration costs, companies have shifted from mail-in sweepstakes to sponsoring online sweepstakes. Internet sweepstakes are easier to run and less expensive to set up than mail-in contests: they are *also* easier and less expensive for people to enter; meaning the company running the sweepstakes will probably receive more entries.

In Canada, mail-in sweepstakes are few and far between. 90% of my entries are online, with the balance split between in-person, call-in, mail-in and text messaging. Companies in the United States are also creating more and more Internet-based promotions; they see a substantial cost savings by running sweepstakes online as well as a greater interaction with their customers. (See section, *Consumer Generated Media*.)

The prizes and experiences you can win from Internet-based sweepstakes are as varied as the sweepstakes themselves. To date, 85% of my wins are from online promotions. I have won everything from CDs, DVDs, movie passes, t-shirts and baseball hats, to a years supply of bubble gum, a set of cookware, running shoes and many vacations. The list seems endless. Basically, anything you could win from mail-in sweepstakes in the past, you can now win online.

81

Early in my hobby I entered an online sweepstakes sponsored by a poultry company. They had an early bird draw (pardon the pun) and my husband won. It was a weekend at the Molson Indy car race in gold grandstand seats, all the chicken he could eat, free t-shirts and hats, plus a hot lap around the track in a pace car. Craig got to drive down Lakeshore Boulevard (in Toronto) at 190 MPH! This was a great win for him because he is a huge race fan.

I have also had the pleasure of meeting Michael Bublé and Sting.

When I began entering sweepstakes online, I would enter every form manually. It was *very* time consuming. When I say time consuming, I mean I spent about eight hours per day entering sweepstakes.

Since I was unemployed when I started entering sweepstakes on a daily basis, I had the luxury of spending hours manually typing out my information into entry form after entry form.

There was also no rhyme or reason to how I tracked the sweepstakes I was entering. Over time I discovered I was making all sorts of mistakes: entering expired sweeps, entering more than once in one entry only sweeps, not entering daily sweepstakes as often as I was allowed, and I am sure I also unwittingly disqualified myself from dozens of promotions. As I learned what I was doing wrong, I knew I had to come up with a system to track the sweepstakes I was entering, when they ended and who in the household could enter. I also really needed a method to enter each promotion faster. These two needs—the need to track my entries and the need for a system of entering that didn't take literally my whole day—are what lead me to develop the Internet entry system I describe in this book.

Entering online has two components to it: the software tools and the way you can use those tools to your advantage. I will first discuss and describe the tools, then take your through my step-by-step online entry system.

My Internet Sweeping System was created, adjusted, and expanded to its current format over a six year period. It has changed over time because new technologies have emerged and new software packages have been introduced, and as I integrated tips and tricks I received from fellow sweepers. As I stated before, experiment and *have fun!*

> *"Use all the tools available to you."*
> *W. Clement Stone*

SOFTWARE FOR ENTERING ONLINE

Soon after I started sweeping, I noticed people in various online groups chatting about RoboForm, an auto-form filling software package. At first I hesitated to use it because I was afraid if I used form-filling software my entry would be disqualified. Sometimes sweepstakes rules state if you are found to have used an automated sweepstakes entry service you would be disqualified. A paid sweepstakes entry service is very different from auto-form filling software. (See section, *Is This Legal?*) I also had a fairly slow computer without much memory, and adding another program just might have crashed my system.

By December of 2002, though, it had become apparent my computer had even become too slow to run our business. So, I broke down and bought a new computer and wow, was it fast! I could get through my sweepstakes in much less time. I started thinking about the auto-form filling software again. I emailed a few people in my online group and was assured using a form-filler would in no way would disqualify me, so I downloaded RoboForm. *It cut my sweeping time in half!* I was hooked.

NOTE: As with any new software package, integrating form filling software into your daily routine does take time to set-up and to adapt to the intricacies of the package. At first, it may seem to be slower. Be patient during this process—it will pay off many times over.

In 2005 I found another timesaving software package: RoboForm Companion. It uses the Passcards in RoboForm to auto-enter form based sweepstakes. It was recommended to me by Tom Stamatson of About.com. He found it very useful so I thought I would give it a try. WOW! Again, my sweeping time was cut in half.

NOTE: I enter the same number of online sweepstakes as I used to, except now I only spend an hour or two per day sweeping since I started using programs such as RoboForm and RoboForm Companion, as opposed to the three or four hours I used to spend.

Other sweepers *love* using Sweep and Sweepstakes Tracker because of their ability to track sweepstakes entries. This can be especially helpful if the promotion is one entry per person or household for the entire entry period. Most sweepstakes will disqualify you for duplicate entries and many promotions do not use Repeat Entry Blocks. (See chapter, *The Other Side of a Sweepstakes*.)

Some sweepers *love* using the entry tracking systems offered on several sweepstakes websites such as: Contest Girl, Hypersweep or Sweepstakes Today. (See section, *Websites*.) The benefit of using a Web-based system is, if you travel and do not have a notebook computer, or would like to enter from multiple computers, you always have access to your sweepstakes wherever you can access the Internet.

As I have mentioned before, I have based my system around RoboForm and RoboForm Companion, but don't take this as my saying that these programs are *better* than other entry systems or methodologies— experiment, try different programs and packages for yourself, and determine which approach you like best. *Remember: make this hobby your own.* The important thing is to take advantage of computers to do what they do best: doing the same thing exactly the same way over and over again really *really* fast. Let them do the tedious repetitive tasks so you can concentrate on the important part: entering more sweepstakes!

To maximize the number of entries you can submit on any given day, I recommend you use one or more time saving software packages. It was through talking to others and taking advantage of free trial offers that I came to know about and love the various sweeping tools I currently use. All software packages can be removed from your computer if you do not find them useful.

NOTE: Most of these packages offer a free trial period. If you like a package, buy it. Buying a software package you like and use every day is worth every penny. I believe it is good karma to support the software developers if the package helps you. (See chapter, Attracting Luck.) It will also encourage them to design and create newer and more innovative software to keep up with ever evolving sweepstakes entry forms. Support those who make good tools, and they will support you back.

Is This Legal?

The sweepstakes rules sometimes state an automated entry is illegal. My original fear was that form filling software would be considered an automated entry and I would be disqualified. This is not the case because you are entering the sweepstakes from *your* computer. The system cannot tell if you manually typed in your personal information or a form filler did it for you. All it does is save your fingers from retyping the same data over and over again.

A company can detect if you are using form filling software only *if* they enable the database to log time-related information. If they choose to check they would be looking at your IP address, how much time you spent on the entry page and how much time passes between multiple entries from the same address (e.g. spouse, son, daughter, best friend, etc.) not each keystroke on the webpage.

NOTE: IP address stands for Internet Protocol address and is a unique address/numeric code that certain electronic devices currently use in order to identify and communicate with each other on a computer network utilizing the Internet Protocol standard.

It is up to the sponsor to determine the parameters of disqualification. Some companies do not care how you enter, as long as you do, and others write a very detailed clause in the rules about automated entries and the respective penalties. Again, it is very important to read the rules and look for such clauses.

In any case, what most sweepstakes companies are concerned about isn't whether or not you use software to enter your entry information for you; what they are concerned about is whether you have hired a sweepstakes entry service to enter promotions *for* you using their automated entry systems. Sweepstakes sponsors do not like automated entries because it defeats the purpose of their promotion; to get you excited about their product or service by participating in their sweepstakes yourself. Even using RoboForm Companion does not disqualify you because you are entering every promotion, form by form, from *your* computer. You still need to go to the sweepstakes entry site to set up the Passcard (and to read the official rules, of course...), so the company is still getting your attention. You still see the products they are promoting along with the sweepstakes—the only difference is you're saving yourself some wear and tear on your fingers. Paying an automated entry system company to enter for you is completely different, in that you may never see the promotion or even know which sweepstakes you are entering with those services.

NOTE: Using My Internet Sweeping System (or a similar one) will allow you to 1) enjoy the hobby of sweeping and 2) enter you into far more promotions than a service can provide. I average 6000+ entries per month as opposed to the 1000+ offered by many automated entry system companies.

NOTE: All software packages listed were available at the time of printing; however, some have not been regularly updated. Check www.contestqueen.com for software updates and new programs available. Any prices quoted below were correct at the time of printing and are subject to change.

Sweeping Software

BUPA (Barcode UPC Personal Assistant)
www.emogic.com/software/software/bupa/

BUPA allows you to organize, share, display and print UPC codes. It is a very useful program for those who enter sweepstakes requiring a UPC. This program replaces the many file folders of product packages and UPCs sweepers used to keep. Just enter the UPCs into the software and it is stored for future use. The number is then easily retrieved to be entered into an online sweepstakes form requiring a UPC. If you are entering a mail-in sweepstakes that requires a UPC, you can print out the barcode and either freehand a reasonable facsimile or trace it. This program is free of charge. A donation of $15.00 is appreciated.

Rewards
www.emogic.com/software/freeware/rewards/

Rewards allows you to enter in a sweepstakes URL, how often you would like to enter it and when the sweepstakes is over. To start, select SHOW TO DO. You get a list of what sweepstakes you would like to enter. It is then a matter of going down the list, clicking on GO TO SITE, filling out the entry form, clicking MARK AS DONE then NEXT TO DO. It is very easy to use. To auto-fill forms, you can use RoboForm in conjunction with Rewards. This software is free of charge. A donation of $15.00 is appreciated.

NOTE: Once you launch Rewards, click on REGISTER. You will then get an INVALID CODE message. Click PROCEED to enter the program.

RoboForm
www.roboform.com/?affid=im123

NOTE: Type in the code QUEEN to receive a 10% discount when purchasing RoboForm.

RoboForm is a password manager and a form filler software package. It completely automates the password entering and form filling process. It does this by allowing you to add in Identities with all of the data usually found on online entry forms (such as Name, Address, Telephone Number, Birth Date, etc.). When you open a webpage that has a form RoboForm can fill, a pop-up window appears with all your Identities. You can then select a name (Identity) and fill the form with one click.

If a form has many more fields, such as a short survey, you can fill in the entire page and save it as a Passcard; every time you return to that particular webpage, you can fill the whole entry with just one click. Passcards also memorize the URL of the form that you have filled. This allows you to use the GO FILL toolbar command or the GO TO in the Passcard Editor to navigate your browser to that web page with the sweepstakes entry form and automatically fill the form from the Passcard.

RoboForm also has a portable version called RoboForm2Go that resides on a USB memory stick, which allows you to take your Identities and Passcards with you everywhere. This is especially helpful for the sweeper who does not have their own computer and must rely on family, friends or the public library for computer/Internet access. You can also purchase RoboForm for your Palm or Pocket PC.

RoboForm works on most pages except those built with Flash. It can also be used to speed-up the data entry of forms that have verification codes, are part of a two-step entry process or have multiple frames on the page. (See section, *Using a Form Filler to Enter*.)

RoboForm offers free online tutorials for you to get familiar with their software at www.roboform.com/tutorials.html.

RoboForm Pro is $29.95 and $19.95 for RoboForm2Go. There is a 30-day money back guarantee and all future upgrades are free of charge.

NOTE: The free version of RoboForm will only allow you to have ten Passcards. If you choose to use RoboForm Companion in conjunction with RoboForm, you will need to buy RoboForm Pro. (I have an average of 250+ Passcards I use within RoboForm Companion at any given time.)

RoboForm Companion
www.cydrix.com

RoboForm Companion was created in 2002 by Vincent Lavoie, CEO of Cydrix Solutions. His brother and father are sweepers and needed an easier way to submit their forms. With his programming experience, knowledge of the Internet, and understanding of a sweeper's mentality, he was able to create a program that works hand-in-hand with RoboForm.

As with any new software package, it took me a few days of playing around with RoboForm Companion to understand how it would work best for me. I now use RoboForm Companion to enter every sweepstakes that uses form-based entries. The only sweepstakes that I can't use it for are those that use certain types of password fields, agreement pop-ups or are designed in Flash, it will not work. (See section, *Using Auto-Submit Software to Enter*, for further information on how it fits into my daily routine.) I continue to go to those types of entry forms daily and fill them out manually. (See section, *Using an Internet Browser to Enter*.)

NOTE: Sweep or Sweepstakes Tracker are similar software packages. The one difference is that Sweep runs over a standard web browser like Internet Explorer, whereas Sweepstakes Tracker has its own integrated web browser.

Sweep
www.wavget.com/sweep.html

Sweep allows you to keep detailed records of all the online sweepstakes, contests and promotions you enter electronically. Once launched, it opens a small window over Internet Explorer. You record the start and end dates of the promotion and how often you can enter along with any notes/comments such as UPCs. Sweep will also track your number of entries into a given sweepstakes. This package is very good for someone wishing to keep all of their online sweeping information in one place. Sweep is free of charge.

NOTE: RoboForm also works in conjunction with Sweep.

Sweepstats
www.sweepstats.com

Like me, Janice Bodinet combined her background and her hobby. Janice has been a database administrator for over 20 years. When she became a sweeper and prizes began arriving in the mail, she wanted a quicker way to find the sweepstakes information rather than digging through mounds of paper. She originally wrote Sweepstats for herself to keep all her sweepstaking information organized. Janice found Sweepstats so useful she thought she should make it available for others.

You can track sweepstakes information in numerous ways, including the prize, judging agency, sponsor, name of sweepstakes, entry method and ending date range. You can also track your wins vs. entries. There are statistical reports you can print that tell you what percentage of your wins are from various sweeps categories. These reports also assist you during tax time calculating your total wins and your total number of entries. (See chapter, *Tax Implications*.) Sweepstats is $19.99.

Sweepstakes Tracker

www.sweepstakestracker.com

Sweepstakes Tracker is an organizer for handling all aspects of sweepstaking, including online and mail-in entries, your wins and your expenses. Sweepstakes Tracker handles an unlimited number of sweepstakes with an unlimited number of entrants per sweepstakes. With each sweepstakes, you can specify the entry frequency (such as once, daily, weekly, month, quarterly and yearly). It also tracks the number of entries in a sweepstakes and the date of your last entry, plus it automatically reminds you the next time an entry is needed in a sweepstakes. It can be configured for manual or automated entry with automatic form filling.

Sweepstakes Tracker has powerful sorting, filtering and data grouping capabilities to view your sweepstakes, along with customizable layouts allowing you to easily switch between views. Also, user definable categories for sweepstakes, wins and expenses allow you to organize their sweepstakes in any way you wish. These features are extremely helpful if you have a large number of sweepstakes. Additional features include an integrated calendar and web browser.

Finally, Sweepstakes Tracker allows you to record all your wins and expenses. A graphical view of your expenses and wins per category is available plus you can export the information to external programs. This feature is very helpful at tax time. (See chapter, *Tax Implications*.)

Sweepstakes Tracker is available either as a six month subscription for $40 or as an annual subscription for $65.

NOTE: RoboForm also works within Sweepstakes Tracker if you do not wish to use their Entrants feature or if you want to use Passcards.

TypeItIn
www.wavget.com/typeitin.html

TypeItIn is a form filler software package. It increases productivity and accuracy while filling out forms on the web, answering emails, processing orders, and many other tasks where you frequently type the same information over and over again. TypeItIn works with most programs, including word processing applications, remote desktop windows, and many more. In other words, it is not limited to your web browser.

Simply put the text cursor where you want TypeItIn to type by clicking with your mouse. Then click the button in TypeItIn, and TypeItIn will type in the text assigned to that button. Unlike most form filling software, this program works by stuffing characters into the Windows keyboard buffer, so programs cannot tell the difference between a person typing and TypeItIn.

Posting to Groups
http://tinyurl.com/

This is a very handy tool for sweepers. You can take a very long URL and shorten it down. You would want to use this site when posting messages to online groups because sometimes a URL may become unclickable when it "wraps" within the message. This saves others viewing the message from having to cut and paste the URL in their browser or figuring out another way to get to the entry page. It will also save you time when others do the same for you.

EXAMPLE:

Before:
http://www.thestar.com/NASApp/cs/ContentServer?pagename=thestar/Render&inifile=futuretense.ini&c=Page&cid=990761496952&pubid=968163964505

After:
http://tinyurl.com/laxs

For Apple Macintosh®

Until 2006, there was no form filling software packages on the market for Mac users. Sweepers entering on Macs had to either fill in every form manually or use the AutoFILL or auto-complete feature (usually included with the Internet browser).

1Password
http://1passwd.com

NOTE: Go to https://agilewebsolutions.com/store?d=QUEENBOOK to receive a 25% discount when purchasing 1Password.

1Password is currently the only password manager and form filling software available for Macs. You create Forms and Identities similar to RoboForm's Passcards and Identities.

1Password integrates into all the popular Macintosh browsers including Safari and Firefox. After creating your initial identities, 1Password can fill all of this information with a simple mouse click. If you have web pages where you enter sweepstakes on a regular basis, you can save the form and restore it the next time you enter a sweepstakes on that webpage.

In addition to form filling, 1Password can manage all of your online passwords by saving them in a secure database. When it comes time to login to a web site, simply restore the login form. You never have to remember or type a password again.

A free trial version is available for download and grants unlimited functionality for 30 days. After 30 Days, it limits you to 20 saved forms until you purchase a license for $29.95.

TIP: For Apple users with an Intel processor in their Mac, you may consider adding VMware Fusion or Parallels and a PC operating system. This way you can run RoboForm and RoboForm Companion as well as 1Password and have the best of both worlds.

"Luck is what happens when preparation meets opportunity."
Seneca

MY INTERNET SWEEPING SYSTEM

The secret to any system is *consistency*. I enter sweepstakes *every day*, 7 days per week. Remember: to win prizes on a consistent basis, you need to enter on a consistent basis. (There are some odd days I don't enter any sweepstakes due to a busy life but they are few and far between—and I *always* make sure I go back to sweeping as soon as possible if I do miss a day.)

On average it takes about 90 days before you begin to win because the sweepstakes you enter today will not be drawn for a few weeks. Don't let this potential lag discourage you—keep entering, and the wins will come. Also, you could enter an instant win sweepstakes online and win TODAY!

This section assumes a working knowledge of computers and basic software packages. If you are new to computers or would like to learn more about computer basics, I recommend reading Windows for Dummies. (*Be sure to read the book relating to the version of Microsoft Windows® on your computer.*) I will give you a brief overview of my system followed by detailed examples.

Each step in the online entry system is designed to build one on top of another. That way as you get more comfortable entering online the learning curve required to make an addition or change will be shortened.

NOTE FOR MAC USERS: The Internet Sweeping System is almost the same. The software for Macs is called 1Password, (see section, Sweeping Software) but the techniques of finding sweepstakes, entering them efficiently, and tracking your entries is the same as for Windows users.

Firstly, ensure you have an email account that you only use on sweepstakes entry forms. You can either set one up with your Internet service provider or you can use a free web-based service (e.g. Hotmail, Yahoo or Gmail). Since more and more websites are requiring passwords with at least one capital letter and one number, create your password for sweeping containing one of each type of character from the beginning. Use the same username and 6+ character password for all your online sweepstakes entries at this beginning level. As you integrate software you will see that they have the ability to generate and save stronger unique passwords.

NOTE: For security reasons, do not use the same username or password for personal or business use—that way, if someone gets your sweeping username and password, they can't also use it to access your bank accounts.

Using Your Internet Browser to Enter

When I started sweeping online, I began by just saving the online sweepstakes I came across into a folder called Sweepstakes under Favorites in my online browser Microsoft Internet Explorer® (IE).

NOTE: FAVORITES allows you to save and organize webpage addresses (also called URLs, which stands for Uniform Resource Locator). You can use this sweepstakes organization system in the Netscape, Firefox, Opera, or Safari browsers using Bookmarks and Folders. Other browsers use the term "bookmark" where Internet Explorer calls them "favorites," but regardless of the naming they all allow you to save URLs so that you can go back to the website later.

As I stated previously, as my list of sweepstakes to enter grew, I began to get confused as to when a sweep ended and how many people in the house could enter. I found myself making mistakes, such as entering sweeps that had already closed. That is how my folder system began.

I created three folders with obvious names:

- Daily
- Weekly
- Monthly

As I found new sweepstakes I would go to the entry page and read the rules to determine end date, number of entries per household and the entry period. I would then save the URL to the appropriate folder with the end date, a new name, and the number of people I could enter.

94

NOTE: I enter One Time Entry Only sweepstakes as soon as I find them and forget about them. You can set up a "One Time Entry" folder if you elect to enter those sweepstakes later in the entry period or you wish to use it to remember which ones you have already entered.

TIP: Enter Daily sweepstakes every day, Weekly sweepstakes on a specific day of the week such as every Monday, and Monthly and One Time Only sweepstakes on the first and/or the fifteenth of the month. That way you will always remember when to enter.

Let me review the system in more detail. Have your three (or four) folders set-up in your Favorites before you begin saving sweepstakes links and bring them to the top of your list. I will use a non-sweepstakes site for this example as real sweepstakes sites can change on a daily basis.

For example, you are watching TV, reading a magazine or receive a link via email advertising sweepstakes whose grand prize is a trip around the world. You decide to check out the sweepstakes and type the sweepstakes URL into your web browser, www.contestqueen.com.

The **first thing** you do is **read the official rules**. There are several things you are scanning for:

- the sweepstakes entry period (e.g. June 1, 2008 to December 31, 2008);
- the region the sweepstakes is open to (e.g. open to all residents of the United States);
- age restrictions (e.g. persons who are the age of majority or more within the state in which they reside);
- how many people per household can enter (e.g. one entry per person or email address);
- how often you can enter (e.g. once per day, once per week, etc.);
- any other requirements or restrictions specific to that sweepstakes.

If you do not meet all of the sweepstakes requirements, even if your name is drawn you will not win. I cannot stress the importance of this enough—I have disqualified myself many times in the past because I rushed reading the rules.

Once you have determined the sweepstakes criteria, save the link in the appropriate folder. For our example, suppose the sweepstakes is running from June 1, 2008 until December 31, 2008, is open to all residents of the United States who are the age of majority or more in the state in which they reside, and allows one entry per household per 24 hour period. CLICK on the STAR with the PLUS SIGN, then on ADD TO FAVORITES. A window will pop-up with a Name and Create In folder list.

TIP: You can either leave the name as it appears in the field; "Contest Queen" or you can change it to something you would remember such as "Around the World Trip".

Type the end date of the sweepstakes (YY-MM-DD format) followed by sweepstakes name and the number of entrants, **08-12-31 Around the World Trip 1PH.** SELECT the Sweepstakes Daily folder in the Create in window and click on OK. Now, when you are in IE and you select FAVORITES, the Daily folder and you will notice your new shortcut to the sweepstakes entry page has been added to the bottom of the list. Select it and move it into end-date order, with the sweepstakes ending soonest at the top.

NOTE: 1PP equals one entry per person and 1PH equals one entry per household.

TIP: Having your sweepstakes in end-date order will allow you to enter those that are ending shortly first. This is important for the days you may not have as much time to sweepstakes so you can get the most entries in as possible per sweepstakes.

As the sweepstakes end dates arrive, enter the sweepstakes and delete the link on the last day. If you are sweeping on a consistent basis you will always have an evolving list of sweepstakes to enter. Since companies are moving away from mail-in sweepstakes to online sweeping, I always have a list that has no less than 50 sweepstakes at any given time—I have had it as large as 200+. To delete a sweepstakes, use the right mouse button and click on the sweepstakes link you wish to remove. A pop-up menu will appear. Select DELETE, and when prompted CLICK the YES button. If you accidentally delete a link, you can always retrieve it from your Recycle Bin if you haven't emptied it.

TIP: When reading the rules, also check the TIME the sweepstakes ends. Frequently, it will end at 11:59am, not 11:59pm, which means you only have until Noon the last day to get your final entry in.

TIP: This system does not record what sweepstakes you have entered in the past once it has been erased from your Favorites. If you want to track what you have entered, you can use a notepad or a program like Sweepstakes Tracker, or you can move the sweepstakes to another folder (such as "Completed").

To avoid confusion when entering more than one person into a sweepstakes, always enter everyone in the same order. (e.g. yourself, spouse, sister, brother, daughter, son, etc…)

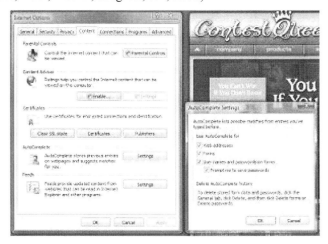

*TIP: Ensure AutoComplete is activated in IE. In IE, CLICK on TOOLS, INTERNET OPTIONS, CONTENT and in the Personal Information section, CLICK on AUTOCOMPLETE. Ensure Web Addresses, Forms and User Names and Passwords on Form are checked. Then CLICK OK and select MY PROFILE. Go through every TAB and fill in all your personal information. **Browsers for Macs have a similar auto-fill feature.** This feature will enable the browsers to fill in this data for you automatically so you don't have to type it each time—a real time saver.*

One Time Only

I like these sweepstakes the best because I feel the playing field is level since everyone has an equal chance. I may be biased since many of the sweepstakes I have won have been from single entry sweepstakes.

There are two theories to entering these sweepstakes: some people enter as soon as they hear about a sweepstakes and others wait until the sweepstakes has been running for some time. I have tried both over the past several years and I can't definitively say that I have won more one way or the other. You can decide for yourself which way you prefer to enter since your odds of winning are the same either way.

If you choose to enter sometime during the sweepstakes period, your link saving method is almost the same. The only difference is, after you read the rules and discover what the entry period is, select as many dates as you wish to enter for yourself, your spouse, and other family members or friends using their initials as a marker. So using our example from before, the entry would read **08-12-31 Around the World CRW JUN 15 CWB AUG 15 NPW OCT 15**.

This would enter myself (CRW) on June 15 (JUN 15), my husband (CWB) on August 15 (AUG 15), and my daughter (NPW) on October 15 (OCT 15), the various intervals throughout the sweepstakes. After the sweepstakes entry date passes for the first person and they have been entered, use the right mouse button to select the sweepstakes. This will bring up the pop-up menu and select RENAME. Erase the first initials and entry date and click on OK. This will leave it in the One Time Only folder for the next date, when you will enter the next person in the sweepstakes. (See section, *Using a Form Filler to Enter* about adding and using multiple Identities in RoboForm to speed-up entry process.) It is important to remember to remove the names as you enter various people, so that you do not enter anyone more than once and disqualify them.

NOTE: If you enter family and friends into sweepstakes on their behalf, ensure that you have an agreement with them in advance if they win, that they will share the prize with you (e.g. trip for four). I have heard many stories of family members no longer speaking or friendships souring because of something that was supposed to be fun going awry.

Ongoing Sweepstakes

There are websites that always have lists of ongoing sweepstakes. They are usually split into two categories: Daily or Weekly. www.bhg.com and www.quickandsimple.com are good examples of websites that continuously have ongoing daily entries. They are in my Daily folder as: BHG ONGOING and QS ONGOING.

The websites you will want to check on a weekly basis are your local television stations, radio stations and newspapers. The specific websites will vary from city-to-city and state-to-state. Even though most of us can now watch television stations from across the country via satellite/cable or listen to any radio station around the world via the Internet, most small prizes are for local events, or must be picked up in person. As a result, it only makes sense to enter locally. In my Weekly folder I have the links to all the major television stations, radio stations and newspapers in my area. Most sweepstakes are one entry only per person so having them in my Weekly folder allows me to check these sites frequently.

TIP: If you win from a radio station and, for example, their prize policy is you or any one in your household can only win from them once every 30 days, you can add the date of when you can start entering again to the name. e.g. 08-06-30 WKRP

Using a Form Filler to Enter

Once I got a faster computer I began to add sweepstaking software to speed up entering. I discovered using auto-form filling software cut my sweeping time in half, because I no longer had to fill out every online sweeps entry form manually (i.e. type out my personal contact information over and over and over…)

NOTE: The auto-form filling software package I was introduced to first was RoboForm. It is what I started with and what I continue to use. There many other programs that can speed up your online entries. (See section, Sweeping Software.)

Once I added RoboForm it dramatically sped up the time it took me to fill out an online entry form—what I once entered in eight hours, now only took me four! I was now able to fill out the 200+ online entry forms quickly and accurately.

When you first install RoboForm, you will be asked to fill out an Identity. An Identity contains all of the information you need to completely fill a sweepstakes form. When you go to a sweepstakes page with a form, RoboForm launches a small pop-up window with a list of all the Identities you have added to the program. It is simply a matter of selecting the Identity and clicking on either FILL or FILL & SUBMIT. You will then see all the personal data for that person auto-fill on the form.

NOTE: If a sweepstakes page opens and the RoboForm window does not appear, the form is probably in Flash. You will need to type all the data in manually for this type of form each and every time for each and every person. More and more companies are using Flash based forms because: 1) the website can be more interactive, 'hipper', etc. and 2) it slows the avid sweeper down.

Flash is a development environment made by Macromedia (now owned by Adobe, www.adobe.com) for creating web content. It allows developers to add animation and interactive content to a webpage. This matters to us as sweepers because RoboForm and other automated form filler applications will not recognize forms that are written in Flash. If the sweepstakes uses a Flash based form, you will have to enter the data manually. Entering online sweepstakes entry forms based in Flash will increase your time spent entering online sweepstakes because you must manually enter all your personal information.

It is important to note the difference between Fill and Fill & Submit. You will use Fill & Submit when the page is a plain ordinary entry form page. (See section, *Using Auto-Submit Software to Enter* to see how you can speed the Fill & Submit process up even faster!) You will use Fill when the page is not in Flash, but has a two-step entry process, has an authentication code, verification code (aka CAPTCHA) or is in multiple frames, because if you use Fill & Submit you will get an entry error.

NOTE: CAPTCHA is the acronym for **C**ompletely **A**utomated **P**ublic **T**uring test to tell **C**omputers and **H**umans **A**part (http://captchas.net/). *Usually they have a picture of a set of letters and/or numbers that have been distorted in some way and you have to type in that set of characters correctly into a text box in order to complete the entry. Humans can still read them because we recognize the shapes of letters and numbers even when they've been modified heavily; computers, on the other hand, cannot recognize them.*

Always test an online entry form by using Fill first to ensure the form is filled properly and will submit correctly. Once you are sure your entry will be submitted properly, you can use Fill & Submit on subsequent entries. Some sweepstakes have a pop-up agree-to-the-rules feature and you may not be entering properly if you just use the Fill & Submit feature.

Using RoboForm Passcards

RoboForm Passcards can be used in two ways. The first is to use Passcards to more easily fill forms with additional entry fields such as a questionnaire, and the second is to use them as a more powerful version of the sweepstakes filing system described in Using an Internet Browser to Enter.

Within RoboForm you can also create folders to track your entries both by entry period and by person. I have created folders for every person within every entry period naming them: Daily CRW, Daily CWB, Daily NPW, Manual CRW, Manual CWB, etc. Create any other folders you require to match the types of sweepstakes you enter. This strategy is scalable and you can add or delete folders as needed.

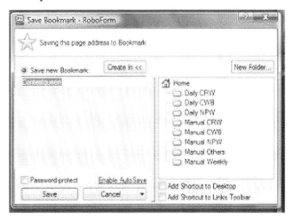

TIP: Separating and submitting your entries in this manner will automatically force some time between them ensuring they are not clumped together on the sweepstakes server.

If you use the same naming system as I described in Using an Internet Browser to Enter, the program will automatically sort them in ascending order. Letters are sorted A to Z and numbers 1 to 9. You can also use your browser to open and edit the folders to delete expired sweepstakes.

You can start by either manually typing all your contact information into the online form, ensuring that all the fields are filled out accurately, or by clicking Identity within RoboForm and then clicking on PASSCARD. A Save Bookmark—RoboForm window will appear for you to name and save the Passcard.

NOTE: The Passcard feature changes its name to Bookmark when you are saving it but it is still a Passcard.

Using the same example as before, I would save the Passcard in the Daily CRW folder in RoboForm as **08-12-31 Around the World Trip CRW**. Even though it is in the Daily CRW folder, I add the CRW at the end of the name in case I make an error and file a Passcard in the incorrect place. If you are only entering for yourself, the initials at the end are unnecessary. Save subsequent Passcards for all the people you would like to enter in their folder: for example, I would save my husband's Passcard in the Daily CWB folder as 08-12-31 Around the World Trip CWB.

Remember to file each Passcard into the appropriate folder for the way it needs to be entered. This is important because if you chose to move to the next step and add an auto-submitting software package, the multi-folder system will make the process easier for you if you pre-separate the ones that are in Flash or have a verification code from those that have plain entry forms.

NOTE: Passcards can also be used with Sweeps or Sweepstakes Tracker.

TIP: You can also add a folder called "Consistent Forms." Many websites that run sweepstakes on a consistent basis use the same basic entry form for all of their sweepstakes, or they may use entry forms that do not fill out correctly if you just click on Identity. So, after you fill out and save the initial entry as a Passcard, save a second copy into the Consistent Forms folder and name it with just the name of the website (for example ContestQueen.com). This saved form never expires unless the website disappears, and you can use it as a starting point for any new sweepstakes that the site runs later. This may seem like a bit more work at first but it will pay off down the road because whenever you need to fill out a new sweepstakes from that website, entry is really simple.

To enter sweepstakes manually, open RoboForm and select LOGINS, EDIT. A new window will open listing every folder and Passcard. Open the manual folder you wish to begin with (e.g. Manual CRW), start at the top of the list and select the first Passcard. Click once. You then have the option to select GO or GO FILL from the toolbar at the top of the screen. If you select GO, RoboForm will take you to that page. This is the option to choose for a Flash-based website. If you select GO FILL, RoboForm will take you to that page and fill all the fields. This is the option to choose if the form has a verification code or two-step entry form that prevents you from entering and submitting automatically. If you click twice (double click) on a Passcard, RoboForm will not only GO FILL, but also submit. If there is a verification code, etc. required, you will get an error message.

*TIP: If a sweepstakes requires a UPC and the entry form is in Flash, you can also add the UPC number right into the Passcard name. For example, for ease of daily entry, you would save the Passcard as; **08-04-30 Trip 0123456789012 CRW***.

Using Auto-Submit Software to Enter

RoboForm Companion is a wonderful software package. It automatically enters any Passcard you have created in RoboForm for plain entry forms (but not those that are built in Flash, those that have authentication or verification codes, have a two-step entry process or have multiple frames) without you needing to do anything. You can walk away from your computer and RoboForm Companion will keep entering sweepstakes for you until it finishes all of the Passcards in the selected folder. This can cut your online sweepstakes entry time dramatically.

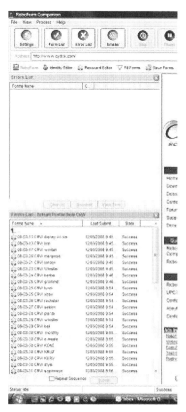

I previously stated adding RoboForm to my daily routine cut my entry time in half. Adding RoboForm Companion cut my entry time in half again! What used to take me four hours to enter now only takes me two. (For those who are keeping track, that means that what used to take me eight hours a day when I was just using Internet Explorer on its own has been reduced to two hours a day—I'm not sure what you can do with an extra six hours a day, but I know I can do a lot! Or, to put it another way, using this system can let you enter four times as many sweepstakes per hour.)

RoboForm Passcards are the secret to using RoboForm Companion. When RoboForm Companion opens, it also opens all the Passcards that have been saved in RoboForm. That's why it is important to 1) purchase RoboForm Pro so you have unlimited Passcards and, 2) learn to use the Passcard feature immediately after learning the basic auto-form fill function on RoboForm. Using Passcards along with RoboForm Companion will greatly speed up your online sweepstakes entering process.

The RoboForm Companion software package is wonderful on days I would otherwise have no time to enter any sweepstakes. In the past, I would not have entered any sweepstakes on days when I'm exceptionally busy, but now I am at least entering what I can with RoboForm Companion. Additionally, once you set RoboForm Companion to submitting all of the Passcards for a folder of sweeps that do not require any intervention; you can leave your computer merrily working away entering contests while you make lunch for the kids.

When you open RoboForm Companion, the first thing you see is your list of folders with your Passcards. Open up the Daily folder you wish to submit and select the Passcards you wish to auto-submit. Once all the Passcards you want to automatically enter have been selected, click SUBMIT and RoboForm Companion will begin entering. Once it has finished entering, close that folder and move on to the next one.

Alternative Online Entry Systems

Sweeps, Sweepstakes Tracker, and TypeItIn are packages I talk about in this book even though I do not use them as part of my Internet Sweeping System. I believe if I had discovered any of these packages earlier, I may have developed my system around one of them instead of RoboForm. Even though I have experimented with different programs and software packages, the others I have tested are very similar to my entry routine and I have felt no need to switch. Try various programs and packages, experiment with various entry methods, find what you like, what is easy for you to use, and have fun!

Remember, hardware and software is ever evolving and so should your online entry system. Experiment with various entry methods, programs and software packages to see if a change makes entering easier and/or increases your wins.

Opt-In or Opt-Out?

Many online sweepstakes entry forms have what is known as OPT-IN or OPT-OUT statements.

Example:

☐ **Yes**, I would like to receive occasional, promotional announcements from ACME Inc.

☐ **Yes**, I would like to receive occasional promotional announcements from Judging Agency Inc., the sweepstakes hosting company.

In most cases, if you click on the box, you are opting-in. If you leave it blank, you are opting-out. Be sure to read the text next to each box in case it is reversed.

Companies use these check boxes to create prospect databases—when you opt-in, you are giving your permission for them to send you information at a later date on their products or services. This *will* result in you receiving email from the company on a regular basis: if you do not want these messages, you should opt-out. However, as the second example shows, many companies offer either advance or start-date notification of new sweepstakes and promotions. If you wish to receive those notifications, you should opt-in. You can always cancel your subscription if you do not like it. Also, the more people that opt-in and the more successful companies feel their sweepstake promotions are, the more sweepstakes they will hold, increasing the number of prizes available.

TIP: Be sure to read the rules, because some promotions require you to opt-in in order to receive an entry into the sweepstakes, while others offer bonus entries.

Consumer Generated Media (CGM)

Consumer Generated Media—also known as User Generated Content (UGC) or social marketing—is growing in popularity with sponsors because creating these types of sweepstakes allows them to interact on another level with their customers. CGM-style sweepstakes ask for the contestant to, for example, create a video for YouTube (www.youtube.com), join a group on Facebook (www.facebook.com) or participate in a game on Second Life (www.secondlife.com). If you are creative and computer savvy, your odds of winning such a promotion are greater because relatively fewer people will put in the effort to win. That said, if there is a voting component, note that it may not be the best entry that wins, but the person with the largest networks of contacts that garners the most votes. Always read the rules to see how the winner is selected before you put the effort in creating something fun and exciting.

Increasing Your Chances

There are many things you can do to increase your chances of winning. The first being **enter as often** as you are allowed. Read the rules to determine what the entry parameters are: once per household, one time per person, daily, weekly, etc. The entry rules will determine how you proceed. This is especially important if a sweepstakes is labeled "per person" because you can then increase your chances by entering your family and friends.

Entering as often as you can goes hand-in-hand with **entering over the entire sweepstakes entry period**. It is especially important to *stagger* your entries over the entire entry period when entering via regular mail because it may be financially prohibitive to mail in entries every day. (See section, *Staggering and Flooding*.)

Look for sweepstakes with **short entry periods**. Sweepstakes that are only open to accepting entries for a two-week period will get far fewer entries than ones that are open for several months.

Promotions with **entry limitations** attract fewer entrants. I have seen sweepstakes limit entries to a city, a zip code, a state and even specific age ranges.

Look for sweepstakes that offer **many prizes** as opposed to, or in conjunction with, a grand prize. On average, they attract fewer entrants so the odds of winning a prize are higher. Also, some of the best prizes we have won were secondary prizes—hey, even if you don't win the car, a new digital camera is always nice.

Some sweepstakes **take time to enter**. Any sweepstakes with qualifiers, specifically mail-in, such as hand-written essays or UPCs, will draw fewer entrants.

Refer Your Friends

Have a circle of sweeping friends—it comes in handy when there are sweepstakes that will grant you bonus entries into the sweeps for referring other people. I have a standard list of ten friends that I use.

Many sweepstakes ask for referrals without granting bonus entries. I only enter friend's email addresses in those sweepstakes that grant extra entries. I also only refer the friends I know will enter. Making friends in the sweeping online communities can help because you know they will enter and increase your odds of winning. (See sections, *Newsletters*, *Sweeping Clubs* or *Websites*.)

There are two types of referral bonus entries: direct and closed-loop. The direct referral will give you a bonus entry into the sweepstakes, just for referring someone. The closed-loop will only give you a bonus entry if the person you referred returns to the website and enters the promotion. This is usually tracked by an email sent to the referral with a unique URL back to the promotion website.

TIP: Remember, it only takes one entry to win!

STORY: This story of how against all odds, in a daily entry sweepstakes, Mary only entered once and WON!

ଶୀଔ

Mary—St. Albert, AB
I couldn't believe my husband and I were going to the Pro Bowl in Hawaii and staying at the Village Hilton! I just wanted to let folks know that even though this sweepstakes could be entered once per day over a four month period, I only entered <u>ONCE</u>. So there you go—keep entering everyone. It only takes one entry. I was also told by the prize

authorities the number of entries was approximately 61,000. So, this one was a 1 in 61,000 win!

ಬುಗ

Time Saving Tips

There are many little things you can do that will save you time entering online:

1. Use the fastest computer you can.

2. Use the fastest Internet connection you can.

3. Use a mouse with a side button you can program to go back to the previous webpage when clicked with your thumb. Or, if you don't have a mouse with this type of button, you can hit the Alt key and the left arrow key on your keyboard at the same time—this shortcut works with Internet Explorer and Firefox, and may work with other browsers as well.

4. Use sweeping software packages such as RoboForm and/or Sweepstakes Tracker.

5. Have two browser windows or tabs open at once and toggle back and forth between them. This is particularly handy when web pages are slow to load.

6. Only enter sweepstakes with prizes you really want to win. It takes as much time to win a car as it does to win movie passes.

7. Only enter the people that will share the prize with you, such as your spouse, child, or best friend.

8. Only enter the required fields. They are usually flagged by a * or are bolded or colored.

9. Only enter online. Mail-in sweepstakes take quite a bit of time to enter in comparison to online promotions.

NOTE: Tip #3 will not work on Flash based websites.

STORY: Rachel relates her tale of how it really does take just as much time to win a car as movie passes. One of the most exciting aspects of this hobby is you never know what you are going to win or when.

৪০03

Rachel—Morrisville, NC

The answering machine message from the bank left my husband concerned. Call the bank back promptly. Did we bounce a check? Did someone steal his identity? As he talked on the phone I walked in. With a quizzical look on his face he turned to face me, "You won't believe this," he said. "We won a car."

A few months prior, I begged him to drive 30 minutes away to a car rental company that was sponsoring a contest for a car along with our bank. I filled out the entries (one per person) and dropped them in the box. My husband, who was skeptical, remained in the car.

Thus, began my hobby of entering sweepstakes and contests. After the first car win, I reluctantly sent off for some miracle water advertised by a local TV evangelist. Couldn't hurt, I thought. After all, he said he had a special connection with The Almighty!

After receiving my miracle water I followed the directions and asked for a win, a few weeks later I won another car. I never told anyone until recently, because I felt like an idiot. After all, who asks God for a win in a contest!

I didn't use the miracle water again; however, I use four leaf clovers in envelopes I put in the mail. I also like using colored envelopes, stickers, cute stamps, fancy postcards and other fun ways to give me "an edge." I have reaped the rewards by winning many sweepstakes.

Every day I find a new contest or sweepstakes to enter. People think I'm crazy until I tell them what I have won. I enter by mail, online or drop box and will often go out of my way to enter for a trip to Vegas.

Recently, a local contest asked for a story regarding a funny bathroom moment. I submitted a poem about my cell phone dropping in the throne. My win….an upscale toilet with all the latest gizmos! "We couldn't stop laughing," the lady at the other end of the phone said.

৪০03

*"Remember, the greatest gift is not found in a store
nor under a tree, but in the hearts of true friends."*
Cindy Lew

JOIN A SWEEPING CLUB

Sweeping clubs have been around in the United States for decades. The Affadaisies are the most famous sweeping club having been featured in both the book and the movie, *The Prize Winner of Defiance, Ohio*.

Like me, Evelyn Ryan, the story's heroine, was elated to discover the best part of entering contests and sweepstakes as a hobby is the people, not the wins. I have made contest buddies, sweeping pals and life-long friends from attending club meetings and conventions.

> Of course, my mother was elated to discover other women out in the world who share her love of contesting. Not that she felt alone in her efforts. She had subscribed for years to the two publications no contester would be without: semimonthly Contest Magazine and bi-monthly Contest Worksheet, both of which announced up-coming contests, rules, and deadlines, and offered helpful hints and essays from consistent winners.

> But Dortha was a living breathing contester, and Mom responded to her letter immediately with the name of the winning entry: My Frisk-the-Frigidaire, Clean-the-Cupboards-Bare Sandwich.

> "Well, no wonder I came in second," Dortha wrote in her next letter. "But I'm proud to say I also came in fourth." (This was true. Dortha had won two of the top four prizes in a single contest.) "My fourth place winner was My Gastro-Comical, Tummy-Yummysome Sandwich," Dortha wrote. "And my absolute favorite

entry-My Ding-Dong-Double-Decked, Left-the-Kitchen-Wrecked Sandwich-didn't win a thing.

"By the way, Evelyn, what did you do with the jukebox? Seeburg has offered me $400 or a color TV instead, but $400 doesn't seem like enough money, and I've already won eleven televisions, so I sure don't need another one."

"Call up Augie Van Brackel," was Mom's advice. "He gave me $500 for my jukebox."

Mom had found a soulmate. In addition to the eleven TVs, Dortha had won thirty-nine radios. And between the two of them, they had seventeen children, hundreds of product labels and box tops (called "qualifiers," or "quallies," in the contest biz), and a single approach to life: "No matter how many kids you have," wrote Dortha, "I'm firmly convinced that a person can find the time to do the things they want to do, and you must want to contest.

"Come to the Affadaisies meeting at my house the first Tuesday of every month," she wrote. "We trade entry blanks, "quallies," and fish stories about the "won" that got away. You'll love it, and besides, I'd love to meet you."

Reprinted with the permission of Simon & Schuster from *The Prize Winner of Defiance, Ohio: How My Mother Raised 10 Kids on 25 words or less* by Terry Ryan. Copyright © 2001 by Terry Ryan

The original clubs in 1957 were The Versatillies based in Fort Wayne, IN and The Affadaisies based in Payne, OH. They met once per month in each other's homes, finding it helpful to consult each other improving their entries. In 1980, due to dwindling members they merged both clubs into The Affadaisies. Sadly, two of the original members are no longer with us: Betty Schmidt and Betty White.

The five remaining members of The Affadaisies celebrated their 50th Golden Anniversary and still meet on a monthly basis. I was lucky enough to attend a meeting and interview the current members.

L-R: Betty Schmidt, Dortha Schaefer, Alice Bruns, Betty Yearling, Maureen Kennerk and Maria Miller.

Alice Bruns
Alice, a friend of Dortha's, attended one club meeting and was hooked! She still enters every contest she can find.

Alice's favorite wins are two sets of World Book encyclopedias and four tickets to the Indianapolis 500. She also loves all the little things she won such as: watches, radios, mixers, coffeepots, etc.

Maureen Kennerk
Maureen joined the Affadaisies in 1980. Dortha read an article about her, discovering they had a mutual love of contesting.

She began entering on the cusp of the hobby making the switch from contesting to sweepstaking. She prefers contesting to sweepstaking as it challenges her and enters all she can find. Her favorite wins were a trip and a car!

In 1978 Maureen spent three weeks listening day and night to a local radio station to identify 20 history heroes. She then mailed in 1000 postcard entries and won a Fiat Spider.

In 1992 she figured out where a virtual treasure was buried. Maureen wrote her 500 word entry in rhyme winning her a one week trip for four

113

to Hawaii plus a rental car, $500 spending money and $500 in food vouchers.

Maria Miller

Maria is the youngest and newest member of The Affadaisies. She met Dortha in 1987 when she was a freelance writer at the same local newspaper Dortha wrote for. Dortha not only encouraged her to join The Affadaisies, but follow her dream of becoming a writer.

Maria, an avid photographer, puts all her talents to use and also enters photography and essay writing contests. She has enjoyed numerous small wins, mainly cash prizes.

Dortha Schaefer

Betty White won a car for entering a last-line limerick contest and talked Dortha into attending a meeting. The hobby was very addictive for her and she enjoys entering to this day.

Dortha was so addicted she would even go to the city dump to "quallie hunt." (Get entry qualifiers such as box tops and can labels to be able to submit more entries.)

Her best win was a jukebox. The best part of the win was making lifelong friends with Evelyn Ryan. She also won 11 TVs and 39 radios!

Betty Schmidt

I was not fortunate enough to meet Betty as she had passed away by the time I met The Affidaisies. Dortha really loved the photo as Betty had been a part of the club since the beginning and wanted to include her and her wonderful memory here.

Betty Yearling

Betty S. invited Betty Y. to her a meeting. At first Betty Y. didn't want to participate but Betty S. "kept on her" until she got hooked on the hobby. She only enters contests, not sweepstakes.

Her funniest win was a pony. Since they lived on a farm they kept him until he began chasing the sheep so they, sadly, sold him. In 1961 Betty won a trip to Brazil but since she was about to have a baby and couldn't travel she was able to convince the sponsor to sell the trip for her. Her most famous win was being a finalist in the 1964 Pillsbury Bake-Off.

Here is Betty's winning recipe for your enjoyment:

Party Pork Barbecue
Bake-Off® 15 (Los Angeles, 1964)
Mrs. C. E. Yearling ~ Payne, OH

NOTE: Three cups leftover pork roast may be substituted for the pork shoulder.

¼ cup Pillsbury BEST® all purpose flour
½ teaspoon salt
1/8 teaspoon pepper
1½ lb. boneless pork shoulder, cut in bite-size pieces
3 tablespoons cooking oil or shortening
1½ cups chopped celery
1 medium onion, sliced and broken into rings
1 cup (8-oz. can) undrained pineapple tidbits
1 cup catsup
½ cup water
2 tablespoons chopped green pepper
2 tablespoons prepared mustard
1 tablespoon Worcestershire sauce
1 teaspoon salt

Drop Biscuits
1 cup flour*
1½ teaspoons baking powder
½ teaspoon salt
½ teaspoon celery salt
¼ cup shortening
1/3 cup milk
1 slightly beaten egg
1 tablespoon dry onion flakes
2tablespoons mushrooms, chopped, if desired
* If using self rising flour, omit baking powder and salt in biscuits.

Heat oven to 400°F. Combine flour, salt and 1/8 teaspoon pepper. Coat pork pieces with flour mixture. Brown well in oil in large skillet.

Add celery, onion rings, pineapple, catsup, water, green pepper, mustard, Worcestershire sauce and salt. Cover;

115

simmer 20 to 30 minutes or until meat is tender. Pour into 2-quart casserole. Drop biscuit mixture (below) by rounded tablespoonfuls onto meat mixture. Bake at 400°F for 20 to 25 minutes until golden brown.

Drop Biscuits
Combine flour, baking powder, salt and celery salt. Cut in shortening until particles are fine. Add milk, egg, dry onion flakes and mushrooms. Stir only until all dry particles are moistened.

Make sure you don't miss out and join or start a club today!

Chosen to Clap and Cheer
by Harriet Brown
From Contest Hotline

February 1st, 1984 was a day I'll never forget. Consider this:

- My friends and I woke up in the luxurious Universal Hilton as guests of *Hour Magazine*. (Where we had seen Telly Savalas in the lobby when we checked in the day before.)
- I had my hair done by Nancy Walker's hairdresser.
- We parked practically next to Gary Collins in the CBS parking lot.
- I found my name on the dressing room door.
- I shared the makeup room (and subsequently the studio audience) with Ricky Schroder and Lauren Hutton.
- We all ate brunch with Gary Collins in the "green room".
- My contesting segment was taped for the *Hour Magazine* show with the very nice, very handsome Gary Collins

And then…

- We drove to NBC to see Johnny Carson – and got front row seats! Johnny's guests that night were Tom Jones and a comedian by the name of Kelton. It was a wonderful, wonderful show.

Now, I would have enjoyed a day like the above even if I was alone, but it was made much more special by being able to share it with Clarice, Barb, and Lucille, three lady friends who flew out to California with me. (I had invited them just two weeks earlier when my husband, and then my sister, decided that now was not a good time for them to make the trip.)

I knew when I invited these friends that this vacation would be extra special—and I was not disappointed. And the promise of appearing on *Hour Magazine* was not the only reason. We are all interested in contesting, in varying degrees, so I knew that having my friends along for support would multiply the pleasure – both for them and for me. True, in this instance I had connections that opened many doors for us, but each person contributed something special to the trip. I didn't know quite how to describe how I felt until last Sunday.

Last Sunday in my church, Pastor Ahnquist's sermon included an anecdote that had a profound message for me—one very appropriate to help me describe the interaction we friends shared. Indeed, it was a message that could be utilized by contest hobbyists everywhere. See if you agree:

Pastor told about a first grade class that was planning to put on a play and only a few speaking parts were needed. On the day the parts were given out, one little boy ran home from school just bubbling with enthusiasm. "Guess what, Mommy, guess what? I've been chosen! I've been chosen to clap and cheer the others!"

A few years ago when Barb won a 15-day trip, a bicycle, a typewriter, and a set of World Book Encyclopedias all within a few months, I did the "clapping". And I clapped again when Clarice won a $1900 Panasonic TV/Video recorder/camera outfit. We take turns winning and take turns clapping and cheering.

117

This is a very real part of the contesting hobby (easily as important as the prizes we win). That is, having friends who will "clap and cheer" us when we win, console us when we lose, and in between times share the myriad of things so important to contestors. That's why I continually stress the importance of having at least one good friend who will share your hobby with you.

Certainly being picked to appear on *Hour Magazine* was a thrilling experience. I felt special and I believe my friends thought I was special, too. At least for the day it was my turn to be in the limelight and their turn to clap and cheer.

Sweeping Clubs

Sweeping clubs meet, on average, once per month at a local restaurant or a member's home. Contact your local club to get specific meeting details.

The sweeping clubs listed are the ones that have agreed to be in this book. There are many more sweeping clubs in the U.S. If you do not see one listed for your area/region, you may find clubs by searching the Internet, within sweepstakes specific websites or attending a convention to meet fellow sweepers from your region.

ALABAMA
The North Alabama/Southern Tennessee Sweepstakes Club
Huntsville, AL
Contact Rebecca at rhoneygtn@yahoo.com or 931.433.2989

ARIZONA
Saguaro Sweepers
Phoenix, AZ
Contact Judy at judygr64@yahoo.com or 480.838.5402

The Southern UT Sweepstakes Club
St. George, Washington, Ivins, Hurricane, Cedar City & LaVerkin UT, Beaver AZ, Mesquite NV & surrounding areas.
Contact Paula at Bubbaadams5@aol.com or 435.986.4156

ARKANSAS
Greater Memphis Sweepers
Eastern AR, Northern MS & Western TN
Contact Karen at rcichon350@aol.com

CALIFORNIA
The Central (Fresno) CA Sweepers
Fresno, CA
Contact Arlene at am385@cvip.net or 559.439.9490

Inland Empire Sweepers
Fontana, CA
Contact Nadine at nadine13@roadrunner.com or 909.863.0152

San Diego Sweepers
San Diego, CA
Contact Mary at maryk02@san.rr.com or 858.672.3470 or Steve at sdadolf@san.rr.com or 858.451.2130

DISTRICT OF COLUMBIA
Chesapeake Crabs Sweepstakers
Baltimore, Frederick, MD & surrounding areas
Contact Brenda at MDCrab3@aol.com or 301.371.6161

The Metro Sweepers
Washington, DC & MD & VA metropolitan areas
Contact Dana at dana_noga@yahoo.com

FLORIDA
Central Florida Sweepstakers
Orlando, FL & surrounding area
Contact Ann at ladylucknov@bellsouth.net or Kathy at matkat80@cfl.rr.com

Sunshine Sweepers
Ocala & Gainesville, FL
Contact Angie at jeepnangie@aol.com

Tampa Bay Sweepaneers
Tampa Bay, FL
Contact Nancy at 5kleins@verizon.net

119

ILLINOIS
The Quad City Winners
Western IL & Eastern IA
Contact Joe at josephrepko@mchsi.com or 309.798.7278

INDIANA
The Hoosier Winners
Plymouth, IN
Contact Deb at djhouin@msn.com

Illiana Sweepers
Hobart, IN
Contact Valerie at kevnval@jorsm.com

IOWA
Central Iowa Winners
DeMoines, IA
Contact Amy at beanieprincess_99_72@yahoo.com

The Quad City Winners
Western IL & Eastern IA
Contact Joe at josephrepko@mchsi.com or 309.798.7278

MARYLAND
Chesapeake Crabs Sweepstakers
Baltimore, Frederick, MD & surrounding areas
Contact Brenda at MDCrab3@aol.com or 301.371.6161

The Metro Sweepers
Washington, DC & MD & VA metropolitan areas
Contact Dana at dana_noga@yahoo.com

MICHIGAN
Eastside Michigan Wolverines
Warren, MI
Contact Al at michigansweepers2002@yahoo.com or 586.791.7819

Flint Area Sweepers
Flint, MI
Contact Patty at pattycollins_2001@yahoo.com or 810.730.9919

Michigan Wolverine Winners
Royal Oak, MI
Contact Al at michigansweepers2002@yahoo.com or 586.791.7819

MISSISSIPPI
Greater Memphis Sweepers
Eastern AR, Northern MS & Western TN
Contact Karen at rcichon350@aol.com

High Cotton Sweepers
North Eastern MS area
Contact Sharon at sharonsheffield@hotmail.com or 662.840.2336

NEVADA
Las Vegas Sweepstakes Enthusiasts
Las Vegas, NV
Contact Linda at lvlp@msn.com or 702.822.1386

Reno Sweepers
Reno, NV
Contact Laura at nwladyspencer@yahoo.com

The Southern UT Sweepstakes Club
St. George, Washington, Ivins, Hurricane, Cedar City & LaVerkin UT,
Beaver AZ, Mesquite NV & surrounding areas.
Contact Paula at Bubbaadams5@aol.com or 435.986.4156

NEW HAMPSHIRE
The Northern New England Sweepstakes Club
Somersworth, NH & ME & MA areas
Contact Jo-Anne at johack@metrocast.net or 603.664.5957 or Pat at
taffy6@metrocast.net or 603.332.4113

NEW JERSEY
South Jersey Sweepers
Mays Landing, NJ
Contact Marge at kittystamp@comcast.net or 609.909.1518

NEW YORK
The Big Apple Sweepstakers
New York City, NY & surrounding metropolitan areas
Contact Steve at animanni1@aol.com

The Lucky Lilacs
Rochester, NY
Contact Terry at tmyoung@rochester.rr.com

NORTH CAROLINA
Carolina Sweepers
Concord & Kannapolis, NC
Contact Sharon at sharonwin1@aol.com or 704.549.1674

Virginia Beach Prize Patrol
Virginia Beach, VA & NC area
Contact Ret at ret2win@aol.com

OHIO
Lucky Bucks
Columbus, OH
Contact Diane at slags68@aol.com

Northern Ohio Sweeps Club
Amherst, OH & surrounding area (*west of Cleveland*)
Contact Rita at sams842@yahoo.com or Nancy at
nmckinney@centurytel.net

OREGON
The Oregon Lucky Ducks Sweepstakes Club
Salem, OR
Contact Mike and Julie at marchison@aol.com or Vickie at
valsetzvic@gmail.com or 503.930.7695

PENNSYLVANIA
Buck County Sweepers
Langhorne, PA
Contact Carol at cmclaughlin528@comcast.net

CenPenn Sweepers
Harrisburg, PA
Contact Patricia at pfnolan17028@gmail.com

Garden Spot Sweepers
Litiz, PA
Contact Cindy at sassycats@embarqmail.com

SOUTH CAROLINA
South Carolina Midland Sweepers
Columbia, SC
Contact Tom at tomfarr77@hotmail.com or 803.328.6689

The Winning Team Sweeps Club
Clemson, SC
Contact Ingrid at ingridjjen@aol.com or 864.646.7391

TENNESSEE
Greater Memphis Sweepers
Eastern AR, Northern MS & Western TN
Contact Karen at rcichon350@aol.com

Music City Sweepers
Nashville, TN
Contact Linda at linda604b@yahoo.com

UcanWin2
Knoxville, TN
Contact Judy at jmcne45379@yahoo.com

TEXAS
Austin Sweepers
Austin, TX
Contact Gail at dgtwight@sbcglobal.net

UTAH
The Southern UT Sweepstakes Club
St. George, Washington, Ivins, Hurricane, Cedar City & LaVerkin UT,
Beaver AZ, Mesquite NV & surrounding areas.
Contact Paula at Bubbaadams5@aol.com or 435.986.4156

UT UPS Chasers
NOTE: Club floats from city to city around northern Utah—approx 80 mile area.
Contact Kim at bargainsfromme@hotmail.com

VIRGINIA
Chesapeake Crabs Sweepstakers
Baltimore, Frederick, MD & surrounding areas
Contact Brenda at MDCrab3@aol.com or 301.371.6161

The Metro Sweepers
Washington, DC & MD & VA metropolitan areas
Contact Dana at dana_noga@yahoo.com

Virginia Beach Prize Patrol
Virginia Beach, VA & NC area
Contact Ret at ret2win@aol.com

WASHINGTON
Puget Sound Clams
Western WA & surrounding area
Contact Jackie at ljackie@excite.com

WISCONSIN
The Fortunate Cookies
Madison, WI
Contact Joyce at tommyjoy66@aol.com

*STORY: Not only can being part of a club bring fellowship into your
hobby and life, it can also bring new adventures, memories and wins.*

ഇരു

Tracy—Burke, VA
Fabio is the Nova Sweeper's sweepstakes idol. We have an 8 x 10
autographed copy of him framed and we draw for it every month at our
meetings. It was originally won by one of our members in an online
instant win game. Whoever wins the photo for the month takes it home
and is guaranteed "Good Luck" for that month. Fabio has brought great
prizes, trips and cash just to name a few. Fabio is sometimes known as
"FABIA" when the men in the group win it. It has been adorned with
coconuts, grass skirts, candied hearts and four leaf clovers. It has been a
great source of luck, fun and laughs!

Fabio has been to several conventions. It was first taken to the
Northeast Mini Sweepstakes Convention at Hershey, PA in 2006. It
brought the member who won him that month lots of nice wins. It has
also attended 18th Annual National Sweepstakes Convention in
Dearborn, MI. There it brought the monthly winner over $500.00 in gift
cards, a Motown CD and some nice sweepstakes supplies.

The Power of Fabio is gaining Nova Sweepers recognition amongst
fellow sweepers. We are happy to share the luck with anyone who

wants to touch our Fabio photo. Of course, you have to believe in order to receive. We are believers.

જીભ્ય

Conventions

The first Annual National Sweepstakes Convention (ANSC) was held in Michigan in 1989. It is run each year by a different sweeping club so the convention moves from city-to-city and state-to-state.

There are heaps of activities at each convention, including featured speakers, raffles, vendors, breakout sessions, road trips, sightseeing, etc. Since each convention is in a new and different location, no two conventions are exactly alike which makes attending every year an adventure.

Further enhancing the experience is the opportunity to meet online sweeping buddies. Putting faces to names, trading winning stories along with tips and tricks are a part of the convention you cannot put a price on.

What also cannot be explained, but must be experienced, is the exhilarating energy of hundreds sweepstakers in one room. Especially, when they have a bag full of freebies and are winning prizes. There is less screaming at rock concerts!

There are also regional events, mini-conventions and even an Annual National Contestors Convention (ANCC) in Canada.

NOTE: For up-to-date convention information, please visit the Resources section of www.contestqueen.com.

Meet Online

Another way to meet fellow sweepers is to join an online group. Being a member of various online communities has also led me to several face-to-face meetings and making real friends. I feel posting sweepstakes and answers has helped me win because it follows the adage *you reap what you sow*. (See chapter, *Attracting Luck*.)

Sweepers may also post when they will be visiting another city on holiday or a business trip. Fellow sweepers will then meet them for a drink at the airport (on a stopover), for lunch, or take them on a tour of their city. I have had the pleasure of meeting many fellow sweepers this way.

You may notice that people participating in the group seem to follow the 80/20 rule. i.e. 80% of the sweepstakes are posted by 20% of the members. Some of the reasons the majority of people do not post sweepstakes are: 1) some members are just better at finding sweepstakes, 2) sometimes someone will go to post a sweepstakes or answer and find that it has already been posted and 3) some members have more time to post sweepstakes and answers.

Not all members will participate in the group. I call those people "lurkers." They enjoy the hobby of sweeping and they learn about all the new sweepstakes and contests from the active members of the group, but they do not give back by posting anything they find or post their winnings. It is impossible to know what percentage of a group are lurkers because you will never hear from them. Don't be a lurker. The enjoyment I get from this hobby is just not the thrill of winning but the joy I get from my sweeping friends. I feel you will miss out on a fantastic part of this hobby if you lurk. (See sections, *Newsletters* or *Websites*, for a list of sweepstaking websites that also host an online group or forum.)

> *"Play fair. Don't hit people.*
> *Say you're sorry when you hurt somebody."*
> *Robert Fulghum*

Online Sweepstaking Etiquette

This section could also be called common courtesy. It is "Do unto others as you would have others do unto you." Since this book's focus is primarily on Internet sweeping, the etiquette will focus primarily on how to behave within an online community, group or forum.

> **Post complete messages**. Before clicking the Send button, review your message to ensure all relevant sweepstakes information is included. You should type a meaningful subject and then include a direct link to the sweepstakes and possibly the rules, what the prize is,

eligibility, how many times one can enter and the end date of the sweepstakes.

EXAMPLE:

New Sweep @ Contest Queen
http://www.contestqueen.com
win a car—open to the U.S.—one entry per person per day—ends Dec 31st
GOOD LUCK,
Carolyn
in Oshawa

TIP: Always include the full URL including the http:// to make the link clickable in the message. Otherwise, one must copy or retype the link in a new window or tab.

Keep your signature file to a reasonable length (4 to 7 lines is usually considered OK). It can be irritating for people to see the same huge signature over and over again. And if your signature includes a picture, make sure it is small so that people who have slow internet connections don't have too much trouble downloading it.

If you post a message and it doesn't appear immediately, please **be patient**. The Internet is not always instant. I have seen the same message posted three and four times because someone didn't give the server a chance to process the original message.

DO NOT TYPE YOUR MESSAGE ALL IN CAPITALS. Not only is it hard to read, it is usually interpreted as shouting. If you can't use the shift key easily, all lowercase is much easier on the eyes and less likely to be misinterpreted.

Most groups and forums will not allow you to send attachments. This is to prevent viruses, pornography, and other unpleasantness from being proliferating to group members, and as a courtesy to members who have slow Internet connections.

127

Do not forward other's postings or messages outside the group without getting permission from the author first. It is rude and inconsiderate, and posting a sweepstakes you didn't originally find to another group is disrespectful to both the group and the poster.

As a follow up to this, if you do need to forward information to a group (or to individuals, for that matter), **delete any email addresses from the original message before you send**. This is a simple courtesy—you wouldn't give out an acquaintance's phone number or home address without their permission, so don't give out their email address either.

NOTE: I post sweepstakes to many groups. However, I only post sweepstakes that I find myself. If another group member found it, I do not cross-post.

Post a Thank You to the group, naming the original poster, when you win something big. People like to be appreciated and to see their efforts of finding sweepstakes are indeed helping others win. It does make a difference.

Online groups and forums are not chat rooms. Do not send one-lined emails, such as "Thank you" or "Good idea". These types of messages should be avoided. When you send a message to the entire group you are potentially sending it to hundreds or even thousands of people. If an email is intended to be read by one particular person, then email that person directly. (Most people show their direct email address either in their message header or signature.)

Before you reply to a posting, **think about whether or not the entire group needs to see your reply**. If your posting is of a personal nature or directed to one person, email them directly.

If you are unsure if your email address is available for others to use when they want to send you a private message, you can **put your email address in your signature file**.

Remove all text that you are not replying too, including headers and signature lines. Extra text makes it difficult to read the reply. Trim quoted text down to just those points you are responding to. Generally, there should be more new text than quoted text. It can be very irritating to read the same message, quoted in its entirety, in dozens of replies. You can assume others have already read the post you are responding to. Remember, you should retain enough of the original message to maintain the context of the topic.

Read ALL emails before replying to one. A subject quickly becomes a "dead horse" when people do not do this.

If you are posting a message that is not about sweeping or *off topic*, please **mark the subject line with either the words Off Topic** or the letters OT.

When entering a sweepstakes that asks for referrals, **do not refer anyone without their permission first**.

Etiquette altered and reprinted with permission from D'Arcy Emery.

TIP: For more Internet etiquette and tips you can go to: http://en.wikipedia.org/wiki/Netiquette or search the Internet using the word "netiquette".

You Can't Win If You Don't Enter

"A snake lurks in the grass."
Virgil

SPYWARE, VIRUSES AND SPAM, OH MY!

One of the biggest concerns or reservations that people tell me they have about entering contests and sweepstakes on the Internet is the possible dangers. They always ask if I get a lot of spam or viruses from entering online. These are certainly valid concerns with some of the nasty computer viruses and spyware running around on the Internet. When you get into the mode of doing a lot of Internet-based sweeping, you simply need to be aware of these hazards and ensure that you have the proper tools running on your machine to keep them out of your computer.

TIP: You should safeguard all your computers against spyware, viruses, spam, etc. regardless of if you are entering online sweepstakes or not. PERIOD. If you are on the Internet, any unprotected computer is vulnerable to these hazards.

NOTE: While much of what you are about to read may sound scary, do not let it prevent you from using the internet for sweeping. Yes there are dangers, but they can be managed. Driving in your car can be dangerous too, but you wouldn't lock yourself in your house because of that, would you?

Terminology

Here are some basic definitions of terms that you should be familiar with when reading through this section:

131

Active X Controls

Active X is technology produced by Microsoft that enables different applications to interact easily with each other. For example, Microsoft Word can be opened in an Internet Explorer browser and specific communications needs to occur between Microsoft Word and Internet Explorer. Sometimes these communication rules are exploited by malicious applications and they can cause harm to your computer.

Browser Hijackers/Browser Helper Objects (BHO)

Browser hijackers are programs that run automatically every time you start your Internet browser. These hijackers can sometimes control your browser, like Internet Explorer. Some Browser Helper Objects are really good for expanding your browser capabilities, but there are others that may not need your permission to install and which can be used for malicious purposes like gathering information on your surfing habits. This can cause anything from incompatibility issues to corrupting important system functions, making them not only a threat to your security, but also to your systems stability.

Data Mining

Data mining is an information extraction activity whose goal is to discover hidden facts contained in databases. Using a combination of machine learning, statistical analysis, modeling techniques, and database technology, data mining finds patterns and subtle relationships in data and infers rules that allow the prediction of future results. For example, people purchasing wood on the Internet would have painting supplies cross sold to them. Typical applications include market segmentation, customer profiling, fraud detection, evaluation of retail promotions, and credit risk analysis.

Drive-by Downloads

A drive-by download is a program that is automatically downloaded to your computer, often without your consent or even your knowledge. Unlike a pop-up download, which asks for consent (albeit in a deceitful manner likely to lead to a "yes"), a drive-by download is carried out invisibly to the user. They can be initiated by simply visiting a website or viewing an HTML email message. Frequently, a drive-by download is installed along with another application.

Keyloggers

Keyloggers are programs that capture and record your every keystroke, including personal information and passwords. They are designed to monitor computer activity to various degrees. These programs can capture virtually everything you do on your computer, including recording of all keystrokes, emails, chat room dialogue, websites visited, and programs run. System monitors usually run in the background so that you do not know you are being monitored. The information gathered by the system monitor is stored on your computer in an encrypted log file for later retrieval. Some programs are even capable of emailing the log files to another location.

Parasites

Parasites are programs that get installed on your computer, which you never asked for, and do some type of activity that you didn't intend for it to do. Almost all the parasites that are currently known are only compatible with Windows, and some only affect the Internet Explorer browser.

Registry Keys

Microsoft Windows stores all of your application information in your registry keys, for example, what software to run, where is the software located, etc. Viruses can manipulate these settings so that applications stop running or run when least expected.

Scumware

Scumware often alters the content of websites you are accessing, changing the normal links to re-route you to other websites. They can also broadcast information that you submit in forms, create more pop-up windows in your browser, and track each and every website that you visit, how long you stay, and which links you clicked on. Most of the time scumware hides itself on your computer in multiple locations to hinder the removal process.

133

Toolbars

Toolbars can be downloaded to your web browser to make browsing easier. Examples are the Google, Alexa, and Yahoo toolbars. Even though these toolbars are very handy to use, they have the ability to track everything you do on the Internet and then pass that information back to the owners of the toolbars. Be sure to read the terms and conditions page before you download any toolbar.

Tracking Cookies

Cookies are small pieces of information that are generated by a web server and stored on your computer for future access. Cookies were originally implemented to allow you to customize your web experience, and still continue to serve useful purposes in enabling a personalized web experience. However, some websites now issue adware cookies, which allow multiple websites to store and access cookies that may contain personal information (including surfing habits, user names and passwords, areas of interest, etc.), and then simultaneously share the information they contain with other websites. This sharing of information allows marketing firms to create a user profile based on your personal information and sells it to other firms. Adware cookies are almost always installed and accessed without your knowledge or consent.

NOTE: Some websites that host sweepstakes on a regular basis use cookies so that when a frequent user returns it is very easy for them to enter a new promotion. If you are using one computer to enter multiple people (family and friends), then you will need to clear the cookies before entering each person. In Internet Explorer this can be done by clicking on TOOLS, INTERNET OPTIONS and DELETE COOKIES.

Trojans

Trojans are malicious programs that appear as harmless or desirable applications. Trojans are designed to cause loss or theft of computer data, and to destroy your system. Some trojans, called RATs (Remote Administration Tools), allow an attacker to gain unrestricted access of your computer whenever you are online. The attacker can perform activities such as file transfers, adding/deleting files or programs, and controlling the mouse and keyboard. Trojans are generally distributed as email attachments or bundled with another software program.

Spyware and Adware

Spyware is any technology or application on your computer that covertly gathers personal information, computer activity or computer content and sends this information to a third party. The data is then sold to advertisers or to other interested parties. The type of information harvested from your computer varies. Some spyware tracks your system information only, such as your type of Internet connection and type of operating system. Other spyware collects personal information, such as detailed tracking of your Internet surfing habits, or worse, the harvesting of your personal files.

Spyware is installed without the user's consent (if you give consent for a company to collect your data this is no longer considered spying, so read online data disclosure statements carefully before consenting). Some people don't object to general spying that track Internet and software trends as long as personal identifying information is not included; others object to any information being taken from their computer without their consent. Either way, the software or device that gathers the information is called spyware.

Adware is considered to go beyond the reasonable advertising that one might expect from freeware or shareware. Typically a separate program that is installed at the same time as a shareware or similar program, Adware will usually continue to generate advertising even when the user is not running the originally desired program. A good example of Adware was a series of products released by Gator, which would just pop-up an installer when you visited certain web sites or pages. The installer would offer you a generally useful utility such as a tool to synchronize your computer clock with an Internet time source; a great tool for those who are not running Windows XP, which already includes this feature. However along with the time sync tool also came a piece of code that allowed Gator to push pop-up ads to your computer. It would also be installed as a separate application from the time sync tool, so you would have to know what the pop-up application was called to completely uninstall it.

135

Adware/Spyware can also simply take the form of website cookies that are left on your machine for tracking purposes. Other sites will see these tracking cookies and know about the other sites that you have visited.

Keep in mind that you may not always get a pop-up or any indication that these applications or cookies are being installed on your computer. Malicious programmers are taking advantage of the many security holes that exist in Microsoft's various Windows operating systems and especially in the Microsoft Internet Explorer browser. Many alternative browsers specifically do not support Microsoft's ActiveX and Visual Basic (VB) Script technologies due to the number of security issues associated with them.

There are a lot of products available now to help you monitor and combat Spyware and Adware on your computer. There are tools that you pay for and free tools that can be installed on your computer, and there are also websites that offer free scanners that you can visit periodically to check your machine. In cases where you are a regular web surfer, it is recommended to have an installed tool on your machine that will proactively check what is happening on your computer and block some of the nastier versions of these applications from getting on your machine in the first place.

NOTE: These tools work much like anti-virus tools and have signature files of known Spyware and Adware technologies. These files need to be updated regularly to combat recent releases of Spyware and Adware on the Internet. Usually these tools have a built-in feature to go and check for product updates.

Anti-Spyware/Adware Tools

While there are dozens of tools available and we recommend that you find a tool that you are comfortable using, we will highlight some of the more popular tools being used below to help get you started:

Ad-Aware
www.lavasoft.us

Ad-Aware is one of the older and better known anti-spyware packages. One unique add-on to Ad-Aware Professional is a built-in popup

136

blocker. This is a wonderful addition for those that would otherwise go out and purchase a blocker. The software also comes with Ad-Watch—Lavasoft's answer to real-time monitoring. Ad-Aware will monitor your Internet activity and warn you if your computer attempts to download spyware or adware; you have the preemptive option to cancel the installation. In addition, you can block ActiveX and web installations to minimize the risk of downloading spyware. It also provides rollback capabilities so you can restore components you may want to keep (deleting some components may disable some desired applications that are dependent on adware). Ad-Aware also comes in three different flavors with increasing features and capabilities. The standard version is free and gives you the basic capability of scanning your system and removing suspected problems.

Ad-Aware has three versions. Standard is free, Plus is $26.95 and Professional is $39.95.

SpyBot Search & Destroy
www.safer-networking.org/en/spybotsd/index.html

SpyBot - Search & Destroy can detect and remove spyware of different kinds from your computer. Spyware is a relatively new kind of threat that common anti-virus applications do not yet cover. If you see new toolbars in your Internet Explorer that you didn't intentionally install, if your browser crashes, or if you browser start page has changed without your knowing, you most probably have spyware. Even if you don't see anything, you may be infected, because more and more spyware is emerging that is silently tracking your surfing behavior to create a marketing profile of you that will be sold to advertisement companies.

SpyBot is free software but they do ask for donations on their site.

Spy Sweeper
www.webroot.com

Spy Sweeper boasts an extensive, easy-to-understand feature set. While scanning for spy or ad components, you can view a progress bar and timer to gauge how long the scanning process is going to take. This product also comes with prevention features that will keep many spyware items from downloading in the first place instead of just removing the offending programs after the fact.

137

By default, Spy Sweeper starts up with Windows and runs in the background to prevent your computer from activating spyware. Spy Sweeper adds new criteria to its search capabilities frequently to ensure that it finds the most recent spyware programs. When a spyware component is found, Spy Sweeper provides a brief description and severity analysis then asks you if you want to quarantine the offending object, where you can delete it. The spyware components found are listed in a tree-like diagram separated into categories that allow you easy, organized inspection. Spy Sweeper even offers a rollback feature that will allow you to restore deleted or quarantined components if you change your mind. The *More Details* button will send you to a website that provides further information on most spyware.

Spy Sweeper is $29.95. A free trial version is also available for download.

Spyware Eliminator
www.aluriasoftware.com

Like many other spyware removers, Spyware Eliminator has the ability to rollback your decisions after deleting spyware—you can change your mind and put that cookie back. Also, the program gives a color-coded severity graph for each spyware component found. When you click on an uncovered spyware program you can read a more detailed explanation of its content. Spyware Eliminator also protects your Internet browser from spyware that would attempt to change your Internet settings.

Spyware Eliminator is $29.95. There is also a free scanner for download.

Free Web-Based Scanners
Both F-Secure and Panda Software offer a web-based scanning option for free which can be found here:

F-Secure – Online Scanner
http://support.f-secure.com/enu/home/ols.shtml

Panda Software Security – ActiveScan
www.pandasoftware.com/activescan/activescan/ascan_2.asp

Malware

Malware is short for MALicious softWARE. It is a generic term increasingly being used to describe any form of malicious software; e.g., viruses, worms, trojan horses, malicious active content, etc. The first form of Malware to evolve was the computer virus. Viruses work and spread (within the infected system) by attaching themselves to other pieces of software (or in the case of macro viruses, documents and spreadsheets), such that during the execution of the program the viral code is executed. Viruses spread across computers when the software or document they are attached to is transferred from one computer to the other.

Computer worms are similar to viruses but are stand-alone software and thus do not require other pieces of software to attach themselves to. They do modify their host operating system, however, at least to the extent that they are started as part of the boot process. To spread, worms either exploit some vulnerability of the target system or use some kind of social engineering to trick users into executing them (such as an enticing email attachment).

Trojan horses are similar to viruses in that they get executed by being part of an otherwise useful piece of software. However, Trojan horses must be attached to the host software manually, and cannot infect other pieces of software the way viruses can. To spread, Trojan horses rely on the useful features of the host software, which trick users into installing them.

A backdoor is a piece of software that allows access to the computer system bypassing the normal authentication procedures. Based on how they work and spread there are two groups of backdoors. The first group works much like a Trojan, i.e., they are manually inserted into another piece of software, executed via their host software, and spread by their host software being installed. The second group works more like a worm in that they get executed as part of the boot process and are usually spread by worms carrying them as their payload.

Anti-virus products are the most common products used to fight Malware. These products are quite mature and have compiled many years of experience in finding and fighting viruses, worms and trojans on your computer. There are two types of anti-virus scans: active and passive. In an active scan, the system monitors and scans the files you use, emails you read and web sites you visit for the existence of a virus or worm. It will then block it from entering your system. A passive scanner is simply a scheduled scan of your system on a daily or weekly basis and does not protect you while you are using the system. Your anti-virus product should have both passive and active capabilities.

Anti-virus/Malware Tools

There are literally hundreds of tools all over the Internet that provide anti-virus features. We will include some of the more popular tools that are widely used and available.

Bit Defender

www.bitdefender.com/index.php

The Live! Update feature checks for product and virus definition updates at either a user-defined interval or manually (default is every eight hours). When you do a manual check for updates, you decide which updates to install. When the software automatically checks for updates, it can update the files at that time or at a time you previously specified during setup.

BitDefender Standard Edition uses the ICSA Labs certified scanning engines, allowing users to feel secure about their virus protection. A very large folder (1.5 gigabyte with over 12,000 files) only took approximately 10 minutes to scan. Bit Defender is $29.95.

TrendMicro's AntiVirus plus AntiSpyware Protection

http://us.trendmicro.com/us/products/personal/antivirus-plus-anti-spyware/index.html

Trend Micro AntiVirus plus AntiSpyware is the essential security you need to safeguard all your data and files. With automatic scans, updates and outbreak alerts, you can rest easy knowing you have systematic, ongoing protection against the latest malicious viruses, worms, Trojan horse programs, and spyware. TrendMicro AV+AS is $39.95 per year.

NOD32 Antivirus

www.eset.com/products

NOD32 Antivirus System provides well balanced, state-of-the-art protection against threats endangering your computer and enterprise

140

systems running various platforms from Microsoft Windows 95/98/ME/NT/2000/2003/XP, through a number of UNIX/Linux, Novell, MS DOS operating systems to Microsoft Exchange Server, Lotus Domino and other mail servers.

Viruses, worms, trojans and other malware are kept out of striking distance of your valuable data. Advanced detection methods implemented in the software even provide protection against the future threats from most of the new worms and viruses.

The fourth generation of the NOD32 Antivirus System features a fully integrated software suite characterized by an unprecedented detection track record, the fastest scanning rates and extremely low utilization of system resources. NOD32 Antivirus is $39.00 and $27.00 per year for updates after first year.

NOTE: Anti-virus/Malware tools rely on signature files that get updated frequently by vendors to be able to keep up with new and changing virus strains that are being released. You should keep your signature files up-to-date to ensure that your computer is protected. Many of these products have a feature to automatically check for updates. This feature should always be enabled and check for updates daily.

Spam

Spam is flooding the Internet with many copies of the same message, in an attempt to force the message on people who would not otherwise choose to receive it. Most spam is commercial advertising, often for dubious products, get-rich-quick schemes, or quasi-legal services. Spam costs very little to send—most of the costs are paid for by the recipient or the carriers rather than by the sender.

Email spam targets individual users with direct mail messages. Spam lists are often created by scanning usenet postings, stealing Internet mailing lists, or searching the web for addresses. Email spam typically cost users money out-of-pocket to receive. Many people—anyone with measured phone service—read or receive their mail while the meter is running, so to speak. Spam costs them additional money. On top of that, it costs money for ISPs and online services to transmit spam, and these costs are transmitted directly to subscribers.

One particularly nasty variant of email spam is sending spam to mailing lists (public or private email discussion forums). Because many mailing lists limit activity to their subscribers, spammers will use automated tools to subscribe to as many mailing lists as possible, so that they cangrab the lists of addresses, or use the mailing list as a direct target for their attacks.

Sweepstakes usually work as a marketing tool and try to include getting your email address. Many of the entry forms that you fill-in will include check-boxes to include or exclude yourself from emails being sent to you outside of the purposes of the sweepstake. You should be vigilant at ensuring that you are excluded from any of these mailing lists to cut down on your exposure to spam. There are still other ways and other sources for marketers to figure out email addresses, so anti-spam software is highly recommended to keep the volumes manageable. (See section, *Opt-In or Opt-Out?*)

Anti-Spam Tools

There is a wide range of anti-spam tools available, and many of them work in different ways to eliminate spam from costing you time and effort in your inbox. Below I will give you a few examples of some of the different styles of spam blocking. It is up to you to figure out which tool works best for your needs.

Be sure to look at the support requirements on the products. If you are using a web-mail box on a large service like Yahoo or MSN, they have spam blocking tools available that you can add to your mail account. For those that use a traditional ISP email account that downloads to your computer from a POP3 source, then you need to match an anti-spam tool to software you use to read your email (e.g. Outlook Express, Eudora, Netscape or Thunderbird).

MailWasher
www.mailwasher.net

MailWasher lets you make a spammer think that your email address is invalid. You can also choose to delete a message on your email server, without downloading it. MailWasher retrieves information about all email messages on the server.

142

To check email, you don't open your email client. Instead, you start MailWasher, and it tells you what messages are waiting for you on the mail server. In the check boxes, you select whether to Delete or Bounce messages, then click the Process Mail button. If you have checked nothing, the email is downloaded to your email client as normal. You can also tell MailWasher to add email addresses to your "friends" list or to your "blacklist"—this will tell MailWasher to always consider the address safe if it is on your friends list or spam if it is on your blacklist. MailWasher will attempt to recognize whether emails are safe or spam based on their similarity to messages that have be processed in the past. MailWasher has two versions: the Standard is free and the Pro is $37.00.

SpamCombat
www.glocksoft.com/sc/index.htm

SpamCombat uses a powerful set of filter rules to prevent spam from entering your inbox: Whitelist, Blacklist, HTML Validator, DNSBL filter, and the Bayesian filters. The Whitelist and Blacklist are the standard lists where you can add conditions to automatically mark an email as good or spam. The messages can be whitelisted/blacklisted based on any words from the message header and/or body, and on the sender's IP address. SpamCombat is provided with a solid Blacklist, which allows you to catch the most known kinds of spam and virus emails. The DNSBL filter consists of comparing the senders' IP addresses against lists of known spam databases using Public Blacklists (also called DNSBL lists). These databases are maintained and updated daily.

The Bayesian filter is the most powerful Spam filter based on the analysis of the message content and mathematical calculation of spam. The advantage of the Bayesian filter is that the filter can be trained by each individual user by categorizing each received email as either spam or good; after you categorize a few emails the filter begins making this categorization by itself. If the filter makes a mistake, you re-categorize the email; the filter learns from its mistakes. The accuracy of the Bayesian filter increases with time. A "well trained" filter can determine up to 99.5% of spam emails coming into your inbox.

SpamCombat is free (single mail account only); or $29.95 for multiple mail accounts.

SpamNet
www.cloudmark.com/products/spamnet

This product integrates with either Outlook or Outlook Express, and gives you access to a community of over one million spam fighters. Install in minutes and forget about it. SpamNet starts working immediately without any configuration or hassle. Every time you block a spam message that slips through, your vote benefits the entire community. Typically dozens of people will vote a spam message as spam long before you go to download it, so this tool can be very effective at keeping spam from hitting your Inbox. Can be configured to automatically delete spam, or quarantine it for your review in case a good message gets caught. You can unblock and white-list addresses of newsletters and mass mailings that you want to make sure you receive. SpamNet is $39.95 per year.

Pop-Ups

Another annoying technology when surfing the Internet is Pop-Ups, Pop-Overs, Pop-Unders and various other advertising techniques that throw extra browser windows at you for things you probably aren't interested in. This technology is thankfully starting to fade. Most web browsers and common browser add-ons now include pop-up blocking features. Some of the products that we mention above include pop-up blockers. Yahoo and Google offer Microsoft Internet Explorer add-on Toolbars that provide pop-up blocking as a feature. You should enable this feature to prevent pop-ups on your system.

TIP: Some sweeping sites may rely on the pop-up technology to be operational on your browser. If you are clicking on something over and over without any results, try turning the pop-up blocker off and clicking again. Remember to re-enable your pop-up blocker after you have finished with that website. Some more advanced pop-up blockers will allow you to create a list of sites where you want pop-ups enabled, this can eliminate the need to remember where to turn the blocking capabilities on and off. Also, many pop-up blockers can be bypassed with a keyboard combination,(usually CTRL ENTER) allowing you to open pop-ups on a case by case basis.

"I've found that luck is quite predictable.
If you want more luck, take more chances.
Be more active. Show up more often."
Brian Tracy

YOU'RE A WINNER!

Typically, you will be notified of a win by one of the following methods: by telephone, email, courier, or mail. Most of my sweepstakes win notifications have been by phone. I get notified via mail and email almost evenly, and I have only had a handful of couriered notifications. **(Sometimes, prizes just arrive in the mail. I love those!)**

TIP: Keep a small note pad, pen and calculator by every phone in the house (even with your cell phone) in case you are called. I have interviewed many people who lost out on prizes because they were not prepared!

The Call

The person calling will ask for the potential winner, introduce themselves and their company, usually mention the sweepstakes name (e.g. Escape to Paradise Sweepstakes) and depending on the value of the prize along with what was required on the entry form.

Write down all pertinent information regarding the caller: get the caller's name, company name and phone number. This is important, because if you need to contact the judging agency, sweepstakes management company or the sponsor regarding the sweepstakes, rules, affidavit and release forms or the prize, you need to know where to begin.

One time, I was driving in my car and I took a winning notification call on my cell phone. Obviously, I was not able to write down the name and number of the person I spoke with. Murphy's Law was hard at work on that win. I keep a spreadsheet of all my wins (see sample below) and I know when a prize has taken longer than the standard 6-8 weeks (usually after the end-date of the promotion) to arrive. The only thing I knew was who the sweepstakes sponsor was, so I began there. It took me two weeks to finally speak to the sweepstakes management company. It took a total of sixteen weeks for my prize to arrive. What I do now is let the person know I am driving and I ask them to call me back at an appropriate time.

CONTESTING WINS 2007

Winner	Date	Prize	Where	Value
Craig	02-Jan	Movie Passes - Freedom Writers	Movie Contests	$20.00
Paul	02-Jan	Professor Noggins Card Game	Canadian Geographic	$14.95
Carolyn	05-Jan	Maple Leaf Hockey Tickets	Toronto Sun	$360.00
Craig	09-Jan	$14.50	bowling	$14.50
Carolyn	22-Jan	Movie Passes - Blood & Chocolate	MIX 99.9	$20.00
Carolyn	24-Jan	Two Tickets to the Oshawa Chamber Wine Tasting	Oshawa Chamber	$60.00
Carolyn	26-Jan	Two Tickets to Cabaret U-Mano	MIX 99.9	$120.00
			JANUARY TOTAL	$609.45
Carolyn	02-Feb	NFL Prize Pack	canada.com	$185.00
Carolyn	07-Feb	Love and Sex Party Prize Pack	NOW	$400.00
Carolyn	19-Feb	FunPass to Frazzled to Dazzled Pamper Party Prize Pack	24 Hours	$120.00
			FEBRUARY TOTAL	$705.00
Craig	01-Mar	Coors Light Peak Party Trip for 2 to Banff AB	Coors Light	$3,500.00
Craig	03-Mar	$15.50	bowling	$15.50
Craig	07-Mar	Book - Bang Crunch by Neil Smith	Random House	$20.00
Craig	07-Mar	Two Tickets to Q107 Triumph Party at Hard Rock Café	Q107	$50.00
Jennifer	08-Mar	$500 Sobey's Gift Card		$500.00
Carolyn	09-Mar	BOSE Earphones	Marriott	$99.00
Paul	14-Mar	Four Tickets - Toronto Sportsman Show	MIX 99.9	$80.00
Craig	27-Mar	Movie Passes - Meet the Robinsons	Toronto Sun	$20.00
			MARCH TOTAL	$4,284.50

NOTE: If you would like to download a blank copy of the spreadsheet to track your wins, check the Resources section of my website under Getting Started.

TIP: If you are not ready to speak to the judging agency or company because you are driving, your kids are screaming, you're too nervous and want to calm down, or any other reason, ask them to call you back and give them an appropriate time (don't just say "call me back later," though, because it sounds like you're trying to avoid them—give them a specific range of times). If possible, also get their name and number.

If you are entering others that live in the same household and they are not available at the time "the call" comes in, take a message for the potential winner, again ensuring you write down all the pertinent information. If no one is home, a voicemail message is usually left. However, I have seen official rules state that if they cannot reach a potential winner, they will not leave a message and another name will be drawn.

Depending on the sweepstakes rules, you will either be sent your prize directly or you may have to fill-out, sign and send back an affidavit and release forms before you are able to claim your prize.

The Letter

Letters arrive either via USPS in your regular mail, by registered mail, or via a courier such as FedEx, Purolator, or UPS. The notification usually includes a congratulatory letter along with the affidavits and release forms. You are generally given a few methods to send back the forms: mail, fax, email (after you scan the forms) or by courier. Since we run our business from home, I usually fax them back due to the ease and speed of returning the forms.

TIP: We get our mail in a community mailbox on our street (aka super mailbox), and don't check the one in beside our front door very often. One day I discovered a Purolator flexible plastic envelope stuffed in there. We had no idea how long it had been there.

STORY: Vicki discovered you should check every possible drop off area around your home for winning notifications.

છળ

Vickie—Dallas, OR
If you have home delivery of dairy products be sure and check your delivery box for prizes. Ours is right by our front door and our delivery guy comes Monday morning, so I leave my order slip out Sunday night. One Sunday at 11:30pm I lifted the lid to put my order slip in and noticed a FedEx envelope. I opened the envelope and was notified I had just won $50,000 in a Sony sweepstakes! FedEx had left the envelope sometime between the prior Monday and Saturday. Eeek! I had no idea it was in there. Better than Easter! Woo Hoo!!

છળ

The Email

I have only received one email notifying me of a large win. All my other email notifications are for smaller prizes such as movie passes, CDs, books, etc. Many people are wary of opening emails stating they have won something due to past experience with fraudulent correspondence. (See chapter, *Avoiding Scams*.) A legitimate email will be similar to a phone call. It will contain the sweepstakes name, possibly what you have won, the company name (of either the sponsor or the judging agency) and who to contact. You will usually be asked to respond/reply to the email within a specified period of time to claim your prize. Most people do remember what promotions they have entered, recognize the sweepstakes name and will know if it is a legitimate email. If you are unsure, call the contact at the bottom of the email.

TIP: Ensure you always make and keep a copy of the affidavit and release forms in case the originals are lost in the mail. If you send the forms back by certified mail you have additional proof you sent them back.

STORY: I never count my wins until the month is officially over. Tina sent this great story of why "it ain't over 'til it's over".

ഏരു

Tina—Wapakoneta, OH

It was December 31st, 2003 at about 2:00pm. Wins were good that year. I had won a digital camera, an Alaskan cruise for my daughter, $500 GC for my son, a computer monitor, $200 worth of Craftsman tools for my husband, Joe, a watch, a washer, $250 worth of CDs, a trip to the CMA Awards, about $300 in groceries and a multitude of other small nice prizes. I certainly had nothing to complain about. Still, most of those larger wins had come earlier in the year and I had been having "vibes"... the ones you get when you feel a good win coming on. I said to Joe, "Gee, I thought I would have one more really good win this year." "Well", Joe said, "I saw the mailman go by. I'll go check for you." "Nope, nothing exciting." Ever the unsinkable optimist, I said "But there's still time for UPS or FedEx! It ain't over 'til it's over!" Joe looked at me sympathetically. He was no longer a Doubting Thomas. He knew all too well the thrill of winning, but the year was almost over.

At exactly 4:00pm I glanced out the window just in time to see the FedEx truck come backing up our driveway. My daughter, who was home for the holidays heard our excitement and bounded down the stairs. "Mom, I should have told you. I ordered some CDs from Amazon and had it sent here." Yeah, we all agreed. That was probably

148

it. Then I watched as the driver emerged from the "Lucky Trucky," as it is referred to around our house, with nothing but an envelope in his hand. That was *not* Amy's order from Amazon! It was unleashed excitement after that!

That envelope held the news that I was a 2nd prize winner in the Lysol $50,000 Scholarship Sweepstakes! I had won $5,000 on New Year's Eve!

Now, when my wins come a little slower, that memory picks me up. You never know when that big win is '*just around the corner*'. I remember that snowy New Year's Eve and remind myself that '*it ain't over 'til it's over!*'

૎૏

There are two adages given to the hobby of sweepstaking: the 3Ps and 4Cs. Every sweeper needs **P**atience, **P**ersistence, and **P**ostage and every sweeper wants to win **C**ash, **C**ars, **C**omputers and **C**ruises.

TIP: Before you begin entering sweepstakes that offer international travel as a prize, ensure all the people that would be travelling with you have a valid passport. Travel restrictions have become tighter over the past several years, so now many promotions state in the rules you must have a valid passport to enter.
http://travel.state.gov/passport/passport_1738.html

Prizes, Prizes, Everywhere!

Have you ever won something and thought, "Why did I enter this sweepstakes? I didn't want to win this. What was I thinking? Now what am I going to do with it?"

There are several things you can do with prizes you don't want:

1) You could **share** your win. If you can't use a prize give it to someone you know who would really like, enjoy and appreciate it. (See chapter, *Attracting Luck*.)

2) You could **sell** your win. eBay is a very popular website for selling anything and everything.

3) You could **trade** your win. You could offer the trade at a sweepstakes club meeting or post a message on an online group or website.

4) You could **gift** your win. I know many people save their winnings for the holiday season and give them away as gifts to ease the financial strain on their pocket books.

5) You could **donate** your win. Another option is to donate you prize(s) to various charities. Many companies and organizations ask for new unwrapped items for children of all ages and their families. (See chapter, *Attracting Luck*.)

STORY: Evelyn won a secondary prize she deemed to be "worthless." One man's trash is another man's treasure.

଼ଓ

Evelyn—Queen Anne, MD
It all started with my entering a one entry per person sweepstakes called "It's A Very Shady Xmas" in 2004.

Around February of the next year a package arrived unannounced. Inside were these bright blue, and I mean *bright* blue, sized 10 men's Custom Air Slim Shady (Eminem) Nike tennis shoes and an autographed card. I don't have any one in the family who would be in need of those shoes so I put them away and forgot all about them.

It was nearing Christmas and my daughter was out of work so I gave them to her to sell on eBay thinking she would maybe get a $100 if she was lucky. Well, the auction went up and she kept getting many emails from people to buy them direct. She declined all of the offers so as not to get in trouble with eBay for selling on the side. We watched the shoes slowly click up in price day after day. Finally, the auction time was near and bids had reached $1,800 we were in total shock! This was truly going to be a good Christmas for my daughter as the bills would be paid and there would be extra for presents.

The last few minutes of the auction were very exciting. The counter was climbing on the number of views of the webpage by about 25 every time we could hit the refresh button. Who would have ever thought? Well, when all was said and done, the auction ended at

$3,500!! Can you believe those bright blue shoes went from a *win* to a *windfall*?!

୫୦୯ଓ

"Winning is important to me, but what brings me real joy is the experience of being fully engaged in whatever I'm doing."
Phil Jackson

YOU WIN SOME, YOU LOSE SOME

I wanted to include a different type of story in this book. A story of great excitement, anticipation, disappointment and finally hope.

I received an email stating I was a Grand Prize Contestant in the Coca-Cola® Mac's iCoke.ca/winamini Sweepstakes. At first I thought I won a Mini. I called Craig up from his office to read the email to determine what I had really won while I stopped hyperventilating. What "Grand Prize Contestant" meant, was, I was one of a hundred chosen for the opportunity to go to Paramount Canada's Wonderland (an amusement park north of Toronto) on the following Saturday and participate in a key-turn drawing for a chance to win a 2005 Mini Cooper Classic. 1 in 100 odds of winning a car was really good!

I use, on a regular basis, all the techniques I talk about in the Attracting Luck chapter. Now, all I seemed to do 24/7 was meditate, think or dream about winning the Mini. I went down to the local Mini dealership, studied the key, took a test drive and bought a Mini t-shirt to wear at the draw. I even had my insurance company give me a quote.

The rules stated I was to arrive at the park three hours before the draw. Since Craig and Nicole came with me, we had time to wander the park, look at all the cool sights and have a bite to eat.

At the appointed time, we gathered at the showcase where the draw was being held. The Mini Cooper Classic was up on the stage surrounded by balloons and lit up with spot lights. (New cars can really shine!) The sweepstakes management company representative came out and gave us a brief overview of what was going to take place. There were sixty keys, each in a little box, on the display table. Wait…Only sixty?! It turns out that sixty out of the hundred potential car winners replied with the proper forms and actually showed up for the draw. My odds had just gotten much better!

They would draw a name from the drawing drum, that person would come up, select a box from the table, go to the car, get in the car and see if their key started the engine. If the key started the engine that person would win the car. Potentially, the drawing could end right away if the first person selected the winning key.

They drew the first name. Not me. The fellow went up, selected a box, and tried to start the car. No go. This went on for about ten more people. Then my name was called. My stomach dropped. My hands were shaking. My heart was racing. I somehow managed to make it to the stage without my knees buckling. I went up, shook hands with the sponsors, closed my eyes and prayed my hand would be lead to the right key.

I walked over to the car and got in. A representative from Coca-Cola was in the passenger seat ready to help the sweepers. I put my foot on the clutch. (It was a standard car and the car would not start if the clutch was not depressed even if I had the right key.) I opened the little box and looked at the key. It didn't look like a Mini key. (Was the Classic key different from the standard Cooper and Cooper S keys??) I began to panic. The key wouldn't even go in to the ignition. The representative said she was sorry. If I couldn't get the key in the ignition it wasn't the right key. I didn't win the car.

I got out of the car and was asked to draw the name of the next sweeper. I picked a name from the drum and then turned to go back to my seat. I was so sad, as I walked back to Craig and Nicole. I felt like the biggest loser. I really thought, with all my heart, I was going to win that car. I guess it wasn't meant to be.

We sat in the stands watching to see what would happen. Only about five more names were called before someone started the car. The entire process only lasted about 30 minutes. I realized I was lucky to even have a chance to go up and try because about two-thirds of the contestants didn't even get a chance to pick a key. Also, the young man that won the car didn't even own one. He needed the car more than I did.

I chose to include this particular story because I wanted you to know: 1) I do not win every sweepstakes I enter and 2) I continue to be happy and excited every day about entering sweepstakes, dreaming about the prizes I could win, being and feeling lucky, and just overall passionate about sweeping.

"The only sure thing about luck is that it will change."
Bret Harte

Affidavits and Release Forms

It is important to read the documentation sent to you because you could lose if you do not respond correctly or within the specified period of time. Affidavits and release forms are the legal documents that you and any companions sign stating you agree to, and will abide by, the official sweepstakes rules.

Once, I won a $100 gift certificate and while speaking with the judging agency representative, I discovered my name was the third one drawn. The first two "winners" did not call them back.

*NOTE: The time limit to respond will differ from sweepstakes to sweepstakes, so again, **read the rules** to determine how much time you have to reply. Otherwise, you may forfeit the prize.*

TIP: I have had winning notifications arrive by mail the day the release forms are due back at the judging agency or even several days after. Call them immediately; explain your predicament and you will generally get your prize. Everyone understands that occasionally the postal mail takes longer to arrive than originally anticipated.

STORY: Kevin is my husband's best friend and only entered this sweepstakes with Craig's encouragement. Unfortunately, Kevin won, and then lost because he was unable to respond within the specified period of time set out in the official rules.

₧₧

Kevin—Markham, ON
I work for a Swiss company, and occasionally they need me to go to head office for extended periods of time. Craig saw a sweepstakes from a major software manufacturer that would pay the winner back the

purchase price of any new computers that were bought with their applications installed. I rarely enter sweepstakes, but had recently purchased a new laptop. Craig encouraged me to enter, so I thought "what the heck—a free laptop is very affordable..."

I was on a business trip in Switzerland and due to fly home when my employer asked me to stay an extra three weeks to work on a large project. As (un)luck would have it, the draw took place during those extra three weeks, my name was selected, and the judging agency FedEx'd me the affidavits and release forms. But no one was opening my mail while I was away, so no one in my home realized how important the package was. Two days before the forms were due back, the judging agency left an urgent voice mail on my cell phone—but I also wasn't checking messages while I was away. I finally returned from overseas late on a Friday afternoon and got the messages—too late. It was after six o'clock, and I was unable to reach anyone at the judging agency. At that point, I was so jetlagged and disgusted at the situation I didn't bother trying to contact them again.

And no, the extra three weeks at head office didn't pay back the cost of the laptop…

ଛୠଓ୪

TIP: If you plan to be away on vacation, to avoid losing out on a win, have a close relative or friend check your email, your voice mail and read your mail. You can check your voicemail yourself inexpensively using a service such as AT&T World Traveler (www.usa.att.com/traveler/index.jsp) and your calling card. You can also forward your home phone to your cell phone. You can check your email yourself by visiting Internet cafés and using a web-based mail service (http://services.mail2web.com) or if you are taking your laptop you can seek out Wi-Fi "hotspots" (www.jiwire.com).

*"Of course the game is rigged.
Don't let that stop you—
if you don't play, you can't win."*
Robert Heinlein

AVOIDING SCAMS

You Never Have To Pay To Receive a Prize From a Legitimate Sweepstakes!

I cannot stress this enough!

The only money you may have to pay is the government taxes. Most sweepstakes rules will specifically state that you are responsible for all taxes and any other monies you choose to spend (e.g. spending money on a trip or to upgrade a car). The taxes (e.g. airport and hotel) or the customs and duties (due on a prize won in another country being shipped to United States—see *Tax Implications?),* are payable to the U.S. government and do not go to the sponsor or judging agency.

TIP: When you win a trip, it's a cheap trip, not a free trip. An example of this is when you win the airfare and hotel stay, you are responsible for all other monies spent on the trip: meals, taxis, tours, souvenirs, gratuities, etc. Ensure you budget for vacations if you are entering to win trips.

In twenty plus years of infrequent sweeping and six years of daily sweeping I have only ever had one "winning" phone call asking for my credit card number so I could receive my prize. I told them I knew it was a scam and they promptly hung up. I do get dozens of emails, on a daily basis, informing me I won the lottery in some foreign country. My spam filtering software promptly dumps most of those into my Deleted Folder—that is one way to easily spot a legitimate congratulatory email from a fraudulent one.

A legitimate congratulatory call, letter or email will offer you information that 1) you will probably remember (the sweepstakes

155

name) and 2) contact information you can easily verify (e.g. employee, company phone number, address, etc.) If you are unsure, investigate further by doing an Internet search or contacting the company to verify the sweepstakes information.

If you get one of these fraudulent phone calls, emails or letters, get as much information as you can (in the case of a phone call) and forward the information to the authorities.

Many organizations and companies also offer information to help you spot a scam in moments. The Federal Trade Commission has an online article and a downloadable pamphlet called *Prize Offers: You Don't Have To Pay To Play*.
www.ftc.gov/bcp/edu/pubs/consumer/telemarketing/tel17.shtm
www.ftc.gov/bcp/edu/pubs/consumer/telemarketing/tel17.pdf

The USPS has a webpage devoted to avoiding sweepstakes scams with a downloadable pamphlet called *A Consumer's Guide to Sweepstakes and Lotteries* along with links to other resources.
www.usps.com/postalinspectors/fraud/sweepstk.htm

Let's help end fraud.

The **Internet Crime Complaint Center** (www.ic3.gov) is a partnership between the Federal Bureau of Investigation (FBI) and the National White Collar Crime Center (NW3C). This partnership was created to stop Internet and online fraud including sweepstakes scams.

You can submit your complaint, www.ic3.gov/complaint, or contact the authorities online, www.ic3.gov/contact.

Sadly, many telephone scams perpetrated originate in Canada. The RCMP (Royal Canadian Mounted Police), the OPP (Ontario Provincial Police), the Competition Bureau and the Federal Government set up **PhoneBusters** (www.phonebusters.com) to stop fraud. This coalition was originally intended to stop telephone scams. Due to the advent of the Internet and the globalization of fraud, they not only try to stop all fraud in Canada but work with the authorities worldwide to stop fraud and catch these con artists globally.

You can report any suspicious activity to PhoneBusters at the same toll free number in the Canada or the United States.

156

Toll Free: 1-888-495-8501
Overseas and Local: 1-705-495-8501
Toll Free Fax Number: 1-888-654-9426
Fax Number (Overseas and Local): 1-705-494-4008
Mailing Address: Box 686, North Bay, Ontario P1B 8J8
Email: info@phonebusters.com

If the con-artists are no longer able to dupe people into giving them money, the scams and fraud will stop.

Government Regulations

Sweeping Problems

If you have a problem with a sweepstakes your first course of action is to complain to the judging agency. Most companies are in business to make money. Their objective is to keep their client's customers happy so they will usually do their best to resolve any issues you may have.

The two most common problems you may try to get resolved are problems with the sweepstakes itself (e.g. unclear or conflicting rules, problems with the online entry form, etc.) or when trying to obtain a prize (e.g. the prize is extraordinarily late in arriving, not the prize stated you would receive, etc.)

If you are not satisfied with that resolution, speak to the marketing department of the sponsoring company. The sponsor is paying the judging agency to promote their products and services along with attracting new customers. It's in their best interest to have happy winners of their sweepstakes telling all their friends how wonderful the product or experience was, so usually they will do what they can to solve any problems that come up.

If you are still unsatisfied, the last course of action would be to complain to the government.

Who regulates sweepstakes and games of chance?

Both federal and state governments have jurisdiction over sweepstakes and games of chance.

There are several federal statutes and regulations that prohibit unfair and deceptive acts, activities pertaining to lotteries, and the mailing or broadcasting of certain materials. These laws are enforced primarily by the Federal Trade Commission (FTC), United States Postal Service (USPS), Federal Communications Commission (FCC) and the United States Department of Justice (DOJ).

The states also license and regulate games of chance. All states have statutes prohibiting lotteries, which are generally defined as any promotion requiring all three elements of chance, prize and consideration, unless specifically authorized (for example, state-run lotteries or licensed charitable raffles or bingo).

Federal

If you wish to complain about a promotion, you will need to do so through the Federal Trade Commission (FTC) or the United States Postal Service (USPS).

FTC
Toll Free:
1-877-FTC-HELP (1-877-382-4357)

Mailing Address:
Consumer Response Center
600 Pennsylvania Avenue NW
Washington, DC 20580

Online Complaint Form:
www.ftc.gov/ftc/cmplanding.shtm
Contact Us:
www.ftc.gov/ftc/contact.shtm

You can also forward unsolicited commercial email (spam), including phishing messages (see chapter, *Spyware, Viruses and Spam, OH MY!*), directly to the FTC at spam@uce.gov. These messages will be stored in a database law enforcement agencies use in their investigations.

USPS
Toll Free:
1-877-876-2455

Mailing Address:
Criminal Investigations Service Center
Attn: Mail Fraud
22 S. Riverside Plaza, Suite 1250
Chicago, IL 60606-6100

Online Complaint Form:
http://postalinspectors.uspis.gov/forms/MailFraudComplaint.aspx

State

You would want to contact your local state government to obtain
permits and licenses if you are interested in holding any type of gaming
activity. Many organizations do this (e.g. soccer and hockey clubs,
school and church groups, etc.) when they want to raise money for their
group or club by holding a raffle, casino night or bingo.

Your state's attorney general is also a place you can go to for assistance
if you have a problem with a sweepstakes.

Alabama
www.ago.state.al.us

Alaska
www.law.state.ak.us

Arizona
www.azag.gov

Arkansas
www.ag.arkansas.gov

California
http://ag.ca.gov

Colorado
www.ago.state.co.us/index.cfm

Connecticut
www.ct.gov/ag

Delaware
http://attorneygeneral.delaware
.gov

District of Columbia
http://occ.dc.gov

Florida
http://myfloridalegal.com

Georgia
http://ganet.org/ago

Hawaii
www.hawaii.gov/ag

Idaho
www2.state.id.us/ag

Illinois
http://illinoisattorneygeneral.gov

Indiana
www.in.gov/attorneygeneral

Iowa
www.IowaAttorneyGeneral.org

Kansas
www.ksag.org/home

Kentucky
http://ag.ky.gov

Louisiana
www.ag.state.la.us

Maine
www.maine.gov/ag

Maryland
www.oag.state.md.us

Massachusetts
www.mass.gov/ago

Michigan
www.michigan.gov/ag

Minnesota
www.ag.state.mn.us

Mississippi
www.ago.state.ms.us

Missouri
http://ago.mo.gov

Montana
www.doj.mt.gov

Nebraska
www.ago.state.ne.us

New Hampshire
www.state.nh.us/nhdoj

New Jersey
www.state.nj.us/lps

New Mexico
www.nmag.gov

New York
www.oag.state.ny.us

North Carolina
www.ncdoj.com

North Dakota
www.ag.state.nd.us

Ohio
www.ag.state.oh.us

Oklahoma
www.oag.state.ok.us

Oregon
www.doj.state.or.us

Pennsylvania
www.attorneygeneral.gov

Rhode Island
www.riag.state.ri.us

South Carolina
www.scattorneygeneral.org

South Dakota
www.state.sd.us/attorney

Virginia
www.oag.state.va.us

Tennessee
www.attorneygeneral.state.tn.us

Washington
www.atg.wa.gov

Texas
www.oag.state.tx.us

West Virginia
www.wvago.us

Utah
http://attorneygeneral.utah.gov

Wisconsin
www.doj.state.wi.us

Vermont
www.atg.state.vt.us

Wyoming
http://attorneygeneral.state.wy.us

The National Association of Attorneys General (www.naag.org) members are the Attorneys General of the 50 states and the District of Columbia and the chief legal officers of the Commonwealths of Puerto Rico (Secretary of Justice) and the Northern Mariana Islands, and the territories of American Samoa, Guam, and the Virgin Islands. The U.S. Attorney General is an honorary member.

Telemarketers

If you are afraid of being inundated with telemarketing calls after entering many sweepstakes, don't be. Most companies want their customers and prospects to be happy and will not solicit business in this manner. To stop unwanted calls all you need to do is sign up with the National Do Not Call Registry (www.donotcall.gov) and you will not be contacted. If however, the odd telemarketing call does come through, do not hang up. At your first opportunity to speak, politely ask they remove you from their call list. They are legally obligated to do so if you request it. If you hang up, they will call you back.

You Can't Win If You Don't Enter

"A person doesn't know how much he has to be thankful for until he has to pay taxes on it."
Author Unknown

Tax Implications

In the United States, income tax is due on all winnings. Federal income tax law requires you to report the Fair Market Value (FMV) of all sweepstakes and lottery wins and pay the taxes thereby incurred. The amount you will have to pay is based on your total annual income (including such factors such as state of residence, filing status, other income, expenses, etc.) for the year the prize is received; the total could be anywhere from 20%-40% of the FMV.

NOTE: The fair market value is the price at which the property (or item) would change hands between a willing buyer and a willing seller, neither being under any compulsion to buy or to sell and both having reasonable knowledge of relevant facts.

I will state my #1 sweeping tip again:

Read The Official Rules *and* Follow Them!

It is especially important to look for the prize details and the value given to the prize. You can then determine if you are willing to pay the taxes if you win. If not, do not enter.

TIP: If you really like the prize, for example, an all-expense paid trip for 10 to Paris, but the taxes would be prohibitive, enter and if you win, you can request the judging agency for a partial disclaimer, e.g. making the trip for two instead of 10.

NOTE: To ensure you only pay FMV on your prizes and your taxes are filed properly, consult your local tax specialist or certified public accountant (CPA). They can also give you advice on your specific tax questions.

If the prize is valued at more than $600, then the judging agency is legally required to send the winner a Form-1099-Misc (frequently referred to as a *ten ninety-nine*) reporting the FMV of the prize. If the prize is worth less than $600, you may, or may not, get a Form-1099-Misc. You are still legally obligated to report your winnings when you file your taxes whether or not you receive a Form-1099-Misc. Besides helping you to feel lucky, (see chapter, *Attracting Luck*.) for tax purposes, it is important to track all your wins, and expenses, in a spreadsheet or a software package. (See section, *Sweeping Software*.)

To ensure you do not potentially overpay taxes on a prize, document everything associated with that prize. For example, if you win a big screen TV and you receive a Form-1099-Misc stating its value is $5,000, yet the same week you receive the TV you see it advertised in the local paper for $4,000, you would then show an adjustment in your tax return to reflect the difference and the FMV.

Some people treat sweepstaking as a "business" and subject themselves to self-employment taxes. Most sweepers report income and claim deductions as an "activities engaged in for profit." In the latter situation, the taxpayer must itemize deductions and is only allowed to deduct most miscellaneous deductions (which include sweepstaking expenses) to the extent those expenses exceed 2% of the taxpayer's adjusted gross income for the year. If the activity is classified as a "hobby", because it fails to make a profit in enough years, deductions are allowed only to the extent that there is income from sweepstaking in that year. For example, if you only win $1,000 in prizes for the year, but spent $2,000 entering, you cannot claim a loss of $1,000; however you can cancel out your tax liability for the $1,000 in prizes you won.

Expenses can be such things as postage, envelopes, paper and cards, pens, markers, stickers, etc. You may be able to deduct part of your home computer, your Internet access or your text messaging package on your cell phone. Again, I recommend you speak to your CPA to ensure your deductions are allowable, accurate and do not flag you for an audit.

TIP: Get in the habit of asking for and keeping all your receipts.

It is also your responsibility to pay your estimated taxes, especially on large prizes. If you win a car in January, the judging agency may not send you your Form-1099-Misc until the following January. You are required to estimate how much tax you will be paying on the income of the car and make four payments that year (by April 15th, June 15th, September 15th and January 15th). Failure to pay the estimated taxes can result in a penalty in the form of a high interest rate. You could also experience quite a shock at tax time if you must pay a large sum all at once.

NOTE: Prizes are usually non-transferable. This means the one who wins it, is the one that must accept the prize and the one whose name will be on the Form-109-Misc. This is especially important to note if you are entering to win trips, as the one who wins, must go and can take whomever they wish to accompany them. If they cannot travel then the prize is forfeited.

Internal Revenue Service

You can call the Internal Revenue Service (IRS) directly at 1-800-829-1040 or check their website for further resources.
www.irs.gov/individuals/index.html

Sample Form-1099-Misc
www.irs.gov/pub/irs-pdf/f1099msc.pdf

Estimated Tax Form – 1040ES
www.irs.gov/pub/irs-pdf/f1040es.pdf

When you receive a Form-1099-Misc, Box 3 should be selected indicating to the IRS you are reporting your win as 'other income'. If Box 7 is checked, 'non-employee compensation', contact the judging agency to get a corrected form.

If you enjoy gambling or buying lottery tickets in addition to sweeping, be aware the wins and losses from gambling must be reported separately on your return.

Information on a W-2G - Sweepstakes, Wagering Pools, and Lotteries
www.irs.gov/pub/irs-pdf/iw2g.pdf

Gambling Winning Form – W2-G
www.irs.gov/pub/irs-pdf/fw2g.pdf

Saving to Pay the Taxes

There are a few ways you can save or earn money to help pay the taxes on your winnings:

- Work overtime or get a second job. This option has its own tax implications.
- If the prize is very large such as a car or a house, you can approach your bank for a loan or mortgage, using the prize as collateral.
- Sell some of your tangible prizes (electronics, vehicles) to pay for the taxes on intangible prizes (trips).
- Save your pennies. Some people only spend bills and save all of their change. You would be amazed at how quickly pennies, nickels, dimes and quarters add up to real dollars.

David Bach, author of *Automatic Millionaire*, coined the term The Latte Factor®. The concept is, if you save the money you normally spend on lattes, bottled water, cigarettes, magazines, fast food, etc. you can change your life. Using David's methods, you can easily save enough money to pay any taxes on any prize you win.

You can read more about his ideas and calculate your Latte Factor here: www.finishrich.com/free_resources/fr_lattefactor.php, and read a good article David wrote here: http://finance.yahoo.com/expert/article/millionaire/1287.

*"The best luck of all is the luck
you make for yourself."*
Douglas Macarthur

THE OTHER SIDE OF
A SWEEPSTAKES

INTERVIEWS WITH
JUDGING AGENCIES,
SWEEPSTAKES MANAGEMENT COMPANIES
AND PROMOTION MARKETING LAWYERS

One thing I have noticed over the past few years is sweepers have many questions regarding sweepstakes and their rules. They are debated in newsletters and online groups, yet no one has contacted these companies to find out what the true answers are. I had the pleasure of interviewing some of the best judging agencies, sweepstakes management companies and promotion lawyers in the United States. I interviewed each company separately, and to avoid repetition I consolidated their answers into a virtual roundtable discussion.

The interview questions I used were sent to me by sweepers and are grouped by topic. The questions arose from general curiosity as to how promotions are created, executed and managed, confusion created by poorly designed sweepstakes, and fears sweepers have related to the hobby.

NOTE: Judging agencies are also known as sweepstakes development and management companies, or promotional marketing firms.

Cohen Silverman Rowan LLP (CSR)

Cohen Silverman Rowan LLP (www.promolaw.com) has provided counsel for promotion and marketing legal issues since 1977. The firm

167

helps companies with the legal aspects of promotions from conception through execution and conclusion. I spoke with partner Shelly Rowan who had an insight into the hobby that was slightly different from the marketer's perspective and very educational.

Launchfire Interactive (LF)

Launchfire (www.launchfire.com) is an award winning interactive promotions company specializing in online and wireless contests and sweepstakes, advergames, and viral marketing.

My interview with Launchfire's President John Findlay, was interesting. I was only able to ask John about half of the questions. Many of the Internet questions did not apply because the interactive marketing system they have created eliminated many of the problems encountered by sweepers. None of the mail-in questions applied because their company only handles Internet based sweepstakes.

NOTE: Many sweepstakes have a mail-in NPE (No Purchase Entry) option. Since Launchfire's sweepstakes are all no-purchase, they are not required to have a mail-in option.

Marketing Visions Inc. (MV)

Marketing Visions (www.marketingvisions.com) is a marketing agency that incorporates sweepstakes as part of the campaigns they create for their clients. I spoke with President, Jay Sloofman.

SCA Promotions (SCA)

SCA Promotions (www.scapromotions.com) is a promotional risk management company and is the world's leading provider of prize coverage for contests sweepstakes and games. SCA Interactive also builds and hosts instant win promotions for numerous Fortune 100 companies. I interviewed Lisa Lantz, Vice President of Sales.

Ventura Associates, Inc. (VA)

Ventura Associates (www.sweepspros.com) is a sales promotion agency specializing in prize promotions with extensive expertise in creating and managing all types of sweepstakes, contests and games. I had the pleasure of interviewing Al Wester. Al started with Ventura in 1984 as a junior marketer and worked his way up to General Manager.

NOTE: Although it is no longer in print, you can still find used copies of The Prize Winners Handbook by Jeffrey Feinman, past-President of Ventura Associates, on www.amazon.com.

Do sponsors, judging agencies and management companies discourage sweepstakers?

"Sponsors prefer that their loyal customers, the ones that buy their products or services, enter." **CSR** said. **MV** added, "No, the more people that participate and enter the better."

SCA said, "Companies do not mind sweepers. What they do not like is people that try to circumvent the system to win. In other words cheat."

"I agree." **VA** said. "No one has a problem with someone who is following the rules and entering accordingly. To help prevent cheating, rules are getting more stringent and now going so far to say if someone is discovered cheating, not only will they be disqualified from the current promotion but from all future promotions run by the sponsor."

Why do entry forms require an exact birth date?
Is there a rule or regulation that a contestant must put down their correct age?
Are there any hard and fast rules to the age a contestant can be?

Many people do not like to put down their correct age because they are afraid of identity theft.

"There is no law that requires a sweepstakes sponsor to request your exact birth date on an entry," states **CSR**. She continued, "Some companies like to ask for exact age due to state or federal laws governing their particular industry. This is especially important if the sweepstakes is being sponsored by a liquor company as all entrants must be of legal drinking age in their state. Also, if the promotion is targeted toward a younger audience, the sponsor must adhere to COPPA."

NOTE: COPPA stands for Children's Online Privacy Protection Act. Go to www.coppa.org for further details.

MV said, "There is not enough information requested on an entry form for someone to commit identity theft. Companies, in general, like to request an entrant's date of birth for demographic research to better target future marketing promotions."

LF added, "For the promotions we design we only need to know if someone is of legal age so we do not ask for your specific age, but what age bracket you fall into. For example 18-34, 34-49, etc."

"Remember, you never want to lie on an entry form because if you are selected as the winner, you could be denied the prize." says **SCA**.

When a sweepstakes is "daily" or has "multiple entries", do you group the entries together at the end and eliminate the duplicates? Is it really worthwhile to enter every day?

All of the companies had the same basic answer: enter as often as you are allowed. **MV** said "Yes [it is worthwhile to enter] because it increases your total number of entries in the draw." **LF** agreed, "Yes! Enter as often as the rules state you can. We design our promotions so people can get additional entries every day."

No one lumps their entries together. So remember, enter early and as often as you are allowed by the rules.

Do you really check every email to make sure someone didn't accidentally enter twice in a one entry sweepstakes?

All the companies check for duplicate entries. **VA** stated, "Yes. We always scan for duplicate entries. It is very easy to see if someone entered more than once. It is also easy to catch people that try and alter their information slightly to get in an extra entry. We consider those duplicates also and anyone not found following the rules is disqualified."

MV added, "If there was more than one entry method, we compile all the data then run a 'de-dupe' to ensure someone didn't try to enter more than once via Alternative Methods of Entry (AMOE)."

If someone forgets they entered a sweepstakes, if a warning comes up saying "you have already entered," have they disqualified themselves?

If a warning does not come up, what do you do with the accidental duplicates?

SCA said, "No, they have not disqualified themselves. The polite message is called a Repeat Entry Block (REB). It allows us to block cheaters and prevents the honest contestant from accidentally disqualifying themselves. If a sweepstakes did not install a REB on their Internet sweepstakes entry form and you did enter twice, you would be disqualified."

The reason not all promotions have a warning in place is the added cost to the sponsor.

In the rules, you often see "one entry per person, one entry per email address and one entry per household"—why are they not more specific such as one per household?

This is one of the most frequently asked questions. Usually, the rules are written to satisfy the lawyers and not the contestant: as stated **CSR**, "It's counterintuitive for a lawyer to leave anything out which is why the rules are so specific." **MV** said, "Always take the rule up to the largest common denominator, which in this case is, per household."

Is using a software package to fill online entry forms, such as RoboForm, or even the auto-fill features built into Internet browsers, considered automated entries?

"No," said **VA**. "In our opinion, Auto-Complete and RoboForm are not considered automated entries and you will not be disqualified using those programs. Some individuals may use these programs due to disabilities, to make it easier to enter their information. If you are following the rules you will not be disqualified. However, we can see if you are entering for friends and family. It is pretty obvious in the entry log file when we see several entries in a row and each address is the same, and they are all made within seconds of each other. We know not all five members of the family are using the computer at the same time. Each person should enter themselves into every sweepstakes."

If a family shares the same email address (thesmiths@anywhere.com) and the sweepstakes is one entry per person, how do you scan the files for duplicates because if both

John and Jane Smith entered the only field that would differ is the first name?

All of the sweepstakes administrators search for duplicate entries electronically. **SCA** told me "Duplicate searches are conducted electronically, and then reviewed to ensure compliance with the official rules. The guidelines for duplicate entries would be determined by sweepstakes sponsor and incorporated in the official rules.

MV added "Read the rules. If the rules state one entry per person, it would be OK to enter both family members. If the rules stated one per email address then only one person could enter. That said, most sweepstakes that state one entry per person also state one entry per email address. In this case only one person could enter because they share an email address."

TIP: Each person entering online sweepstakes in a household should have their own e-mail address. Most Internet Service Providers (ISP) will allow you to have more than one e-mail address per account. Also, as I mentioned earlier, there are free e-mail services available from Microsoft, Google, Yahoo!, and other companies that can be used to enter sweepstakes.

What happens if someone enters both a husband and a wife then realizes that the sweepstakes is one entry per household? Do you disqualify both entries or just remove the extra one?

This is a tricky one because as **SCA** stated, "Some sweepstakes are sorted and the duplicate is kicked out so the one entry has an equal chance in the drawing. Some sweepstakes are very specific about duplicate entries and if sorted both would be deleted." **VA** said, "We always scan for duplicates and could disqualify both entries, depending upon the official rules of the sweepstakes in question."

TIP: If you wish to keep track of the sweepstakes you enter, use either a manual log or use a program such as Sweepstakes Tracker. My entry system categorizes sweepstakes according to the number of entries allowed specifically to prevent accidentally entering more often than the rules allow.

Married or common law, is it the same thing when it comes to contesting?

172

All the companies had the same answer. **MV** said, "The marital status of any contestant would not matter unless the rules stated that it did." One entry per household is one entry per household.

If the mother's last name is different than the children's, should she enter the father in as the guardian or can she put her name?

Again, everyone had a similar response to this question. **LF** said, "There are stringent laws regarding children and contesting. As long as the parent or legal guardian gives their permission, it does not matter if the last names are different. This is also becoming more and more common for the mother to retain her maiden name and have it be different than the child's."

It is very common now for a mother to have a different last name than her children. As long as she is a legal guardian (parent) of the child(ren), she can use her name when giving permission for the child's sweepstakes entry.

When the rules state one entry per person or household and it's a mail-in or entry box, how is that enforced?

"All the entries are checked to ensure there are no duplicates." stated **SCA**.

MV said, "It depends on (how) the sweepstakes entries are handled. Typically, received entries are entered into a database and then a random electronic drawing is conducted to determine an eligible winner. In this situation, duplicate entries would be filtered out electronically."

If the rules do not state the number of entries such as one-time only, daily, weekly or monthly, how many entries should a sweeper assume?

My response to all sweepers is to ask the company running the sweepstakes to clarify their rules, although many will refuse to do so during the entry period on grounds of fairness. **CSR** said, "If a company does not specify an entry limit in the rules then you can enter an unlimited number of times. You will usually find the rules limit the online entry option, for example, once per person per day, while the mail-in entry option may be unlimited, stating one entry per envelope."

173

Typically, these restrictions are in place to discourage fraud or programmed entries that could crash the sweepstakes website.

Even though I have seen rules change mid-promotion (although this is generally not permitted, see *The Official Rules*.) to fix errors, **CSR** stated, "It is ill advised for rules to change mid-promotion because if the sweepstakes is open nationally the sponsor would have had to bond and register the promotion with some states, such as Florida, and to go back and update or change the rules would be very difficult." Everyone else agreed.

You will find that sweepstakes run by professional sweepstakes management companies will always have the limitation stated in the rules. If a company chooses to run a promotion without hiring a management company, call or write them asking for clarification and requesting future rules be more specific in all aspects including number of entries.

VA confirmed that by stating, "We will typically put limitations in online promotions because of the relative ease of entering, but certainly not in all promotions. It will ultimately depend on the sponsor's rationale for holding the promotion. For example, if you receive one entry each time you use a credit card to make a purchase, one can't restrict an AMOE-entrant to just one entry per day, since the card holder could reasonably make multiple purchases in a given day. In the end, we just want to give everyone an equal chance."

If the official rules state one entry per electronic address, how does more than one person per household enter a one entry per person sweepstakes?

MV said, "One per electronic address means one per household." An IP or electronic address is different than an email address. An IP address is the address of your computer.

"One of the reasons this rule is used is to prevent cheaters from submitting hundreds of entries into a sweepstakes or an automated entry system company from entering hundreds of their customers into a sweepstakes. It is easy to read any entry log and see which IP address each entry is coming from. If hundreds are coming in from the same location(s) within a specific time frame, those entries can be flagged and potentially deleted from the pool of entries." stated **VA**.

I feel this rule can be unfair because everyone entering from a public library or a large office will also all have the same IP address. I have also discovered that some companies mistakenly use the word electronic address when they mean email address. If you find the rules unclear, contact the sponsor for clarification.

VA added, "You typically won't see teams of people at the library entering the same sweepstakes at the same time. We are looking for large blocks of entries from the same IP address, not entries scattered throughout the entire sweepstakes entry log."

What is the definition of weekly? Someone may enter on a Friday (week one) and then try to enter again on Monday (week two) getting the message "you have already entered this week." Is a week Sunday-Saturday or week to week based to the date and time of the first entry?

MV said, "Read the rules because it depends on the promotion and the start date of the sweepstakes. We outline the weekly dates in our rules so a participant will be very clear on when they can enter."

SCA agreed, "How a week is defined will vary from sweepstakes to sweepstakes, so always read the rules. If the dates are not outlined in the rules, just keep entering on a weekly basis from your first entry."

If the rules do not specify which regions (states, or countries) the sweepstakes is open to, does that automatically mean it's open to everyone everywhere in the world?

"A sweepstakes should always specify the regions it is open to, as some European countries have very stringent laws surrounding Internet promotions." stated **CSR**.

If someone says no to having a company contact them via email or any other means, are they also denying them permission to be contacted if they win?

Companies ask this question because they want permission to market their products and services to you in the future. All the companies had the same answer. **MV** said, "No. The permission is for opt-in lists so the contestant can receive information at a later date. It does not affect the sweepstakes entry." (See section, *Opt-In or Opt-out?*)

NOTE: Remember, there are two schools of thought on this subject and you should decide for yourself which you choose to follow. The first is: to cut down on spam, always opt-out. The second is: if you wish to be notified of sweepstakes and promotions from sites and companies that run them on a regular basis, opt-in.

LF had a very good explanation of opt-in vs. opt-out and the validity of your entry. "Giving permission for a marketer to verify eligibility to win a prize and giving permission for follow-up contact for other reasons are two separate issues."

"By entering, a sweepstakes entrant agrees to abide by the official rules, which includes allowing the sweepstakes manager to contact them if their entry is selected as a potential winner. In fact, official rules usually state that the sweepstakes manager will contact each person to verify that they qualify as a winner."

"Permission for follow-up contact by the marketer is a separate issue and may be applied as an opt-in clause on the sweepstakes entry form."

If a sweepstakes offers a tell-a-friend space on the sweepstakes page, is telling the friend mandatory to receiving an entry into the sweepstakes?

This question got several different points of view. **MV** said, "This is called *viral marketing*. It will depend on the client and what is appropriate for the promotion whether or not we add in a tell-a-friend or referral bonus entry feature to the sweepstakes. **LF** added, "We offer a bonus entry for referring friends, so we encourage referral by rewarding the player with extra entries."

"All promotions with a viral marketing component must ensure they follow the CAN-SPAM Act." **CSR** said. **SCA** reminded us, "Always read the rules to see what benefits or bonuses, if any, telling your friends would give you in the sweepstakes."

NOTE: The U.S.CAN-SPAM Act (Controlling the Assault of Non-Solicited Pornography and Marketing Act) was established in 2003

*and outlines requirements for those who send commercial email, spells
out penalties for spammers and companies whose products are
advertised in spam if they violate the law, and gives consumers the
right to ask emailers to stop spamming them.*
www.ftc.gov/bcp/conline/pubs/buspubs/canspam.shtm

**Many contests have an "optional" questionnaire attached to them.
What if someone doesn't fill it in? Will their entry be disregarded
even though the questions are not compulsory?**
**If a sweepstakes with a questionnaire is a daily entry, do you expect
people to fill out the questionnaire each time or is the first time
sufficient?**

SCA succinctly said, "Optional means optional. No, they would not be
disqualified." **MV** repeated my number one tip, "Always read the rules
to see if the questionnaire is compulsory or optional in the entry
process and enter accordingly."

**Sometimes a website is functional before the actual start date. Do
you erase all entries before that date and someone can come back
and re-enter if they did so previously by error, or do you keep all
entries regardless of entry date?**

A promotion should not be made "live" before the official start date as
outlined in the rules. **MV** explained why this may occur. "Sometimes
an online contest entry page is active before the start date for testing
purposes. We delete all entries received before the start date. If
someone accidentally entered a one entry only sweepstakes before the
start date, they could come back and re-enter."

Everyone else had the same opinion. **SD** said, "Not our contests. If, for
some reason, someone did enter before the start date and time, we
would do what is known as a data dump to clear the database. Again
the rules take priority here—so if they state the contest starts on a
certain date, then all entries from that date are included. It would be
wrong to include anything previous to the start date or anything after
the end date."

SCA said, "We erase all early entries. Surprisingly, there are still some
dishonest people who have been known to scan the Internet for
promotions that are in test-mode and enter. If they happen to win an

instant prize, they demand to be sent the prize however if they don't win, they want the database cleared so they can try again. If you are not following the rules, you can't win. It's that simple."

Are your chances of winning better with online or mail-in? This one leads to a question on the industry in general—Do you think mail-in sweepstakes will disappear in time with Internet sweeping becoming the standard?

This question is a matter of new technology vs. "old school." Everyone had the same answer regarding the odds as stated by **MV.** "The chances of winning are the same for online and mail-in."

There were mixed feelings regarding the disappearance of mail-in promotions and the timeline that would occur in. To state that mail-in contests will disappear would be an over-statement. There are still many benefits of marketing and promoting in the offline world. That said, companies are conducting more and more online contests. As Internet usage continues to increase around the world, marketing over the Internet is also.

CSR agreed, "Mail-in promotions are disappearing but they won't disappear entirely. For example, the state of New York still requires a mail-in option for sweepstakes in certain circumstances where a product purchase serves as one method of entry, as not everyone has a computer or easy access to one and they see it as an equal dignity issue."

How much mail do you get in a single day?

Each company couldn't give me an exact number. Overall, volumes are down due the advent of online sweepstakes. **MV** said, "Mail volume will vary—it can range from hundreds to hundreds of thousands to millions. It depends on the types and number of sweepstakes we run at any given time. The mail volume for a specific sweepstakes will depend on how much a promotion has been advertised."

Do decorated, colored, or odd sized envelopes get drawn more often than a standard #10 envelopes?

SCA said, "No. A colored or decorated envelope does not have a better chance of winning than a plain #10 envelope. There are very few

178

promotions where all of the envelopes are put into a drum. When those occur, the official conducting the draw would not be allowed to look at the drum."

The most common consensus is that envelopes don't really matter because there is no drawing drum. Everything is done electronically. **MV** said, "It doesn't matter since we open the envelopes and enter the information into the database."

VA added, "Each promotion is different. All drawings are based on the official rules. All forms of entry must be included (up to all five entry methods) for each entry to have an equal consideration (chance of being selected)."

NOTE: Several of the companies open your envelope and manually enter your data into the computerized sweepstakes database. This is important since you would waste your time and energy by mailing entries into a promotion that possibly has an Internet entry option and/or decorating and embellishing your envelopes.

How do they actually select a winner from the online entries?
Is it done with a computer program or does an official randomly pick a number?
Is each entry given a number and the winning number is predetermined?

All the companies had similar answers. **MV** said, "We use a software package designed to randomly select the winner(s). Most companies use their own internal legal department or promotional law firm to ensure they are following regulations." **SCA** added, "The winner is selected via a software program that chooses random persons from the pool of entrants. It is worth noting that we have a product called TrueDraw—where we can guarantee without a doubt that the winner was selected in an unbiased selection process."

Why does it sometimes take months to make the drawing and then even more take to award the prize?

"Many companies need to schedule their workload so that not all the draws and prize fulfillment need to be done at the same time. Also, some companies do not purchase the prizes until after the drawings are complete so there is a time delay between the draw and when a winner receives the prize." said **CSR**.

"If the sweepstake had multiple entry methods, such as mail-in and online, it takes time to manually enter all the alternative entries into the online database." added **MV**.

SCA added, "If the sweepstakes was open nationally, it may take a few weeks to get all the entry forms into a single location and confirm the winner compliance."

If it is a "one time" only entry, is there a better chance of winning if you enter early or late in the contest?

It makes no difference to your odds of winning if it is one entry only sweepstakes. Enter anytime during the sweepstakes entry period. **LF** said, "There is no difference if you enter early or later during the sweepstakes entry period." And **MV** stated, "It's like the lottery balls. Some go into the machine first yet the numbers that come out are totally random. Everything needs to be random in order to be fair to all entrants."

If someone is lucky enough to keep winning various sweepstakes, do you discard their name so other people can win, or do you actually let those people win over and over again if they are that lucky to have their name picked?

"Yes they can win more than once." said **MV**. "If the rules state one prize per household and multiple prizes are being given away, then they would only win the prize the first time their name was drawn. However, if their name was lucky enough to be selected from several promotions my company was managing, they would win each prize. We do not discard or disqualify entrants that follow the official rules."

When an essay is required, does submitting it early or late in the entry period influence how it is judged?
Are the entries randomly re-arranged and then chosen and judged?

"The sponsor will generally choose a panel of judges and the criteria on which the entries will be judged would be outlined in the rules." **CSR** said. "All eligible entries will be judged according to the criteria, regardless of when the entry is submitted."

MV added, "Contest, not sweepstakes, experts would usually be hired to oversee the promotion. The contest will outline the criteria that each entry would be judged against. All entries would be judged against those criteria. The entry with the highest score would win the contest."

What do you do with unreadable entries? Do you try to decipher them, or just toss them?
What if an entry says please print your name and address and a person is unable to write due to a disability or a disease?

MV said, "We do everything we can to ensure the winning entry gets the prize. We have had entries in the past where only the phone number is legible so we call the winner. If nothing can be read at all we are forced to throw away the entry and redraw." **CSR** added, "It is the responsibility of each entrant to ensure that his or her name and address is correct and legible."

Thankfully, online promotions have removed this problem, as **VA** stated. "Since more and more entries are online we generally do not have a problem, unless entrants are just entering gibberish or obviously fake names and addresses. In the event of a mail-in entry being selected we usually can get enough information off the entry to contact the winner."

What happens if someone doesn't receive their prize?
How do you ensure all prizes are delivered?

Most companies ship with a carrier that requires a signature so the prizes can be traced if necessary. **LF** said, "We use regular mail for small prizes and courier companies for larger prizes. We have never had anyone contact us to say they have not received their prize."

Smaller prizes are usually sent through the mail and, depending on the value, they may or not be traceable. If you do not receive your prize in a timely manner, contact the sweepstakes management company.

What happens to unclaimed prizes?

This was one of the most interesting questions put forth because each company had a slightly different answer.

VA said, "The rules would disclose this information. If the rules state 'all unclaimed prizes will be awarded via a random draw at the end of the sweepstakes,' then that is what will happen. Otherwise, unclaimed prizes are not awarded and the sponsor need not disclose anything further. Note that this is for instant win-type promotions, where lower value prizes may be available in large numbers (think soft drinks or French fries at fast food restaurants). Sponsors would generally prefer to award all prizes in a regular, random draw-type promotion since part of their rationale to hold a promotion is to generate excitement and goodwill among their customers."

LF said, "We draw ten names for each contest. We start with the first name drawn. If the prize is unclaimed we go to the second name, etc...We have never had a prize go unclaimed, although we have had to contact more than one person on the list before a prize was claimed."

SCA said, "We recommend to include in the rules "unclaimed prizes will not be awarded". If that term is not included, alternate names must be drawn until all prizes are awarded. If the contest is an instant win with the term, the companies sponsoring the sweepstakes do not pre-purchase 100% of the prizes since not 100% are claimed. Many winning mail or email winner notifications are either not noticed or thrown away by the winners."

(I can hear many die hard sweepers gasping at the thought of a large win being thrown out!)

MV said, "We do whatever the official rules of each promotion state. If the rules state all prizes will be awarded, we redraw if a contestant does not claim the prize. If the rules state that unclaimed prizes will not be awarded, then that's what we do."

NOTE: If you are entering sweepstakes, respond to any emails, phone calls or letters you may receive congratulating you on your potential win. They are not a scam. I have won many prizes and discovered while talking with the judging agency that my entry was not the first one selected. I was, however, the first one to respond. (See chapter, Avoiding Scams to determine the difference between a real notification and a fraudulent one.)

If a large prize is won in November, but not received until January, in which year will the Form-1099-Misc be issued?

CSR explained the question very well stating, "A Form-1099-Misc should be issued when the prize is available. For example, in December 2007 you win a trip to the Super Bowl. You attend the Super Bowl in February 2008. You would receive your Form-1099-Misc early in 2009 for your 2008 income taxes because even though you won in 2007 the prize wasn't available to you until 2008. On the other hand, if you won a ski vacation in October 2007 and you had a year to use the trip, November 2007-November 2008, the trip is available to you now so you would receive your Form-1099-Misc early in 2008 for your 2007 income taxes."

VA agreed stating, "You should receive your Form-1099-Misc in January of the year following the calendar year in which you have the benefit of the prize."

Can a win be altered? Such as, if you win a trip for four to Walt Disney World and you have three children can you buy a fifth ticket?

The answers were varied but it boiled down to, *ask*. You never know until you ask.

LF said, "They may alter the prize based on a personal situation. It is up to the discretion of the sweepstakes management company and the sponsor. You have nothing to lose by asking."

"A sponsor can say no but most will be accommodating. Remember, the level that they can be accommodating will be based on the prize. It would be easy to allow you to buy an additional plane ticket to a family trip to Florida but almost impossible to alter an experience-based prize such as a beer company sponsored promotion," added **CSR**.

NOTE: Remember, the cost of all alterations and additions is the winner's responsibility, so only ask if you can afford the change/alterations.

Why do companies still require someone to mail-in a request along with an SASE to obtain the winner's list instead of posting it to the sweepstakes website?

VA said, "This part of the official rules is a holdover from the past when most promotions were mail-in. Some states such as Florida also allowed companies to print the list in a local newspaper to meet its disclosure requirements. Remember, too, that not everyone is comfortable with computers or has reasonable access to one, so this is a more realistic option for them."

"When it comes to luck, you make your own."
Bruce Springsteen

ATTRACTING LUCK

As I participated in online forums, attended club meetings and met a multitude of sweepers, I noticed that some people seemed to win far more than others. What set those people apart? I realized there were seven traits and actions winners possessed and did. They:

1. Think positively.
2. Expect to win.
3. Feel like a winner.
4. Have good *chi* flowing inside and out.
5. Share with others.
6. Don't cheat.
7. Enter, Enter, Enter…

"Whether you think you can, or
you think you can't, you're right."
Henry Ford

Positive Thinking

What is your internal dialogue? Is it positive or negative? Are you always saying, **I can** or, **I can't**? Did you know you *choose* how you talk to yourself? I have met sweepers that say "I never win" or "I am not lucky" and I think "WOW! If you think that way, you definitely won't win."

Change your internal and external dialogue. Use *I am*, *I can* and *I will*. Speak in the present tense as if it has already happened: "I am lucky." "I am a winner." "I enter as often as I can." "I win often." Pretty soon you will find those statements and beliefs coming true, not only when you sweep, but in all aspects of your life.

185

WHO DECIDES WHETHER you shall be happy or unhappy? The answer—you do!

A television celebrity had as a guest on his program an aged man. And he was a very rare old man indeed. His remarks were entirely unpremeditated and of course absolutely unrehearsed. They simply bubbled up out of a personality that was radiant and happy. And whenever he said anything, it was so naive, so apt, that the audience roared with laughter. They loved him. The celebrity was impressed, and enjoyed it with the others.

Finally he asked the old man why he was so happy. "You must have a wonderful secret of happiness," he suggested.

"No," replied the old man, "I haven't any great secret. It's just as plain as the nose on your face. When I get up in the morning," he explained, "I have two choices—either to be happy or to be unhappy, and what do you think I do? I just choose to be happy, and that's all there is to it."

That may seem an oversimplification, and it may appear that the old man was superficial, but I recall that Abraham Lincoln, whom nobody could accuse of being superficial, said that people were just about as happy as they made up their minds to be. You can be unhappy if you want to be. It is the easiest thing in the world to accomplish. Just choose unhappiness. Go around telling yourself that things aren't going well, that nothing is satisfactory, and you can be quite sure of being unhappy. But say to yourself, "Things are going nicely. Life is good. I choose happiness," and you *can* be quite certain of having your choice.

The happiness habit is developed by simply practicing happy thinking. Make a mental list of happy thoughts and pass them through your mind several times every day. If an unhappiness thought should enter your mind, immediately stop, consciously eject it, and substitute a happiness thought. Every morning before arising, lie relaxed in bed and deliberately drop happy thoughts into your conscious mind. Let a series of pictures pass across your mind of each happy experience you expect to have during the day. Savor their joy. Such thoughts will help cause events to turn out that way. Do not affirm that things will not go well that day. By merely saying that, you can actually help to make it so. You will draw to yourself every factor, large and small, that will contribute to unhappy conditions. As a result, you will find yourself asking, "Why does everything go badly for me? What is the matter with everything?"

The reason can be directly traced to the manner in which you begin the day in your thoughts.

Tomorrow try this plan instead. When you arise, say out loud three times this one sentence, "This is the day which the Lord hath made; we will rejoice and be glad in it." (Psalm 118:24) Only personalize it and say, "I will rejoice and be glad in it." Repeat it in a strong, clear voice and with positive tone and emphasis. The statement, of course, is from the Bible and it is a good cure for unhappiness. If you repeat that one sentence three times before breakfast and meditate on the meaning of the words you will change the character of the day by starting off with a happiness psychology.

While dressing or shaving or getting breakfast, say aloud a few such remarks as the following, "I believe this is going to be a wonderful day. I believe I can successfully handle all problems that will arise today. I feel good physically, mentally, emotionally. It is wonderful to be alive. I am grateful for all that I have had, for all that I now have, and for all that I shall have. Things aren't going to fall apart. God is here and He is with me and He will see me through. I thank God for every good thing."

"Luck affects everything; let your hook always be cast. In the stream where you least expect it, there will be fish."
Ovid

Expectations

Do you expect to win? I do. If I go to bed at night and I have not won anything that day I am genuinely disappointed. I am the only person I know that looks forward to Mondays because the judging agencies generally only notify winners during the work week and I can hardly wait for the next winning call, letter or email.

NOTE: We have only once been notified by a judging agency of a win on a Saturday. We have also won online instant win sweepstakes on weekends.

One of Richard Wiseman's four scientific principles of luck is: Expect Good Fortune.

> My research revealed that lucky people do not achieve their dreams and ambitions purely by chance. Nor does fate conspire to prevent unlucky people from obtaining what they want. Instead, lucky and unlucky people achieve, or fail to achieve, their ambitions because in a fundamental difference in how they think about both themselves and their lives.

> Earlier on in the book we met lucky competition winners Lynne, Joe and Wendy. All of them won a huge number of prizes, and all put much of their good luck down to the fact that they enter a large number of

competitions. As Joe said, "You have to be in to win." Many of the unlucky people explained that they never entered competitions and lotteries because they were convinced that their bad luck would prevent them from winning. As Lucy, a 23-year-old unlucky student, told me:

I can remember, even when I was little, not entering things because I just never won anything. When I was seven, I was at primary school in an assembly and my parents were in the audience. My mum had entered a competition for me and they called out the winner and it was me. But I hadn't entered it, it was my mum. The way I see it, I hadn't won, she had.

Clearly, unlucky people's expectations about competitions are very likely to become self-fulfilling prophecies. By not entering competitions, they severely reduce their chances of winning, and exactly the same attitude affects many important areas of their life. The resulting lack of any attempt to change their lives can easily turn unlucky people's low expectations about the future into a miserable reality.

From the book THE LUCK FACTOR by Dr. Richard Wiseman. Copyright © 2003 Dr. Richard Wiseman. Reprinted by permission of Miramax Books/Hyperion. All rights reserved.

"You get what you think about, whether you want it or not"
Abraham

The Law of Attraction

In 2003 a colleague introduced the Law of Attraction concept to me. I found the idea a bit odd at first and the more I read, the more I liked the notion that I could be lucky and be a winner by feeling lucky and feeling like a winner. Since then the book and movie *The Secret* have made the Law of Attraction a household term.

189

You Can't Win If You Don't Enter

We create by feeling, not by thought!

That's right; we get what we get by the way we feel, not by trying to slug things into place or control our minds. Every car accident, job promotion, great or lousy lover, full or empty bank account comes to us by the most elemental law of physics: like attracts like. And since most of us haven't felt too hot about what we've had for most of our lives, we've become highly gifted masters at attracting an overabundance of circumstances we'd rather not have.

You want a new car? You got it! You want to work successfully for yourself? You got it! You want to close that deal? Make more money? Have a great relationship? Live without fear? Have a spiritually fulfilling life? Have superb health, freedom, independence? You got it, *if* you know how to f*eeee*l it into being.

The Law of Attraction—like attracts like—is absolute (and has nothing to do with personalities). No one lives beyond this law, for it is the law of the universe. It's just that we never realized until recently that the law applies to us too. This is the law behind success or failure. It's what causes fender-benders or fatalities. It is, to the point, what runs every waking moment of our lives.

So if we want to turn our lives around, or bring in greater abundance, or health, or safety, or happiness of any kind, we have only to learn the simple steps of manipulating our "feelings," and a whole new world of plenty opens for the asking.

But the greatest obstacle to living our potential comes from toddler days when we were trained to look for what's wrong—with everything! With our jobs, our cars, our relationships, our clothes, our shapes, our health, our freeways, our planet, our faith, our entertainment, our children, our government, even our

190

friends. Yet most of the world can't even agree about what right or wrong is, so we war, and strike, and demonstrate, and make laws, and go to psychiatrists.

"That's life," you say. "We have to take the good with the bad, the ups with the downs. We have to be on guard, work hard, do things right, be watchful and hope for a break. Yes, that's the way life is."

No, no, and NO! That is simply not the way real Life is, and it's time we faced up to how we actually do create what we have in our world, our empty or full bank accounts, our grand or boring jobs, our good fortune or bad, and everything else in this arena we so nonchalantly call reality.

How do we do it? Don't laugh; it all comes from…*how we're vibrating!*

Everything in this world is made of energy: you, me, the rock, the table, the blades of grass. And since energy is actually vibration, that means that everything that exists vibrates. Everything! Including you and me.

Modern-day physicists have finally come to agree that energy and matter are one and the same, which brings us back to where we started: that everything vibrates, because everything—whether you can see it or not—is energy. Pure, pulsing, ever-flowing energy.

But even though there's only one energy, it vibrates differently. Just like the sound that pours out of a musical instrument, some energy vibrates fast (such as high notes) from high frequencies, and some vibrates slow (such as low notes) from low frequencies. Unlike the tones from a musical instrument, however, the energy that flows out from us comes from our highly charged emotions to create highly charged *electromagnetic* wave patterns of energy, making us powerful—but volatile—walking magnets.

That's nice, but who cares? Well, if you want to know why you've had to struggle so hard with your life, you do! If you want to know how to change your life to be exactly the way you want it to be, you had darn well better care, because the electromagnetic vibrations you send out every split second of every day are what have brought—and are continuing to bring—everything onto your life, big or small, good or bad. Everything! *No exceptions.*

Reprinted with the permission of Hampton Roads Publishing Company, Inc., 434-296-2772, www.hamptonroadspub.com, from *Excuse Me, Your Life is Waiting* by Lynn Grabhorn. Copyright © 2000 by Lynn Grabhorn

"The Law of Attraction does not respond to the words you use or the thoughts you think. It simply responds to how you <u>feel</u> about what you say and what you think."
Michael Losier

There are some actions you can take to begin vibrating to attract what you *do* want, as opposed to what you *don't* want.

SELF TALK
A Self Talk is an expression we use as a statement of truth. It can be positive or negative and it often made unconsciously. It can also be called your inner voice.

Negative Self Talk
- I'll have to work hard to make good money.
- I never win the lottery.
- I'll never lose the weight I want.
- Good women/men are hard to find.
- Money comes in one hand and goes out the other.
- It's hard to get clients during the summer.
- I take one step forward and two steps back.
- My business slows down during the holidays.

Complaining and worrying are negative statements. Every time you complain about something, you're giving more attention to what you don't like. When you worry about the future, you're giving more attention to what you don't want.

Positive Self Talk
- ♦ I'm lucky, because I always find money.
- ♦ I always find work and clients easily.
- ♦ Everything I touch turns to gold.
- ♦ I make friends easily.
- ♦ Money comes to me at the right time.
- ♦ I always get a great parking spot.

At this point, you're probably asking yourself how you can stop your pattern of negative thinking. The answer comes in the act of rephrasing what you think and what you say.

HOW TO REPHRASE NEGATIVE SELF TALK
As you become more aware of your use of language and its importance in your vibration, you will begin to catch yourself whenever you make a negative statement. When you hear it, turn the negative into a positive by restating what you have just said. Preface your sentence with "in the past." For example, if you hear yourself say, "It's hard to find clients," rephrase it by saying, "In the past, it was hard to find clients."

Copyright ©2003 by Michael Losier. Used by permission. www.michaellosier.com or www.lawofattractionbook.com

STORY: Carmen shows us how she used the Law of Attraction in her life to attract in wins. The trick is to do all three steps: Ask, Believe and Receive. Most people only do the first two.

ဆာ

Carmen—Norfolk, VA
I'd like to tell you about how *The Secret* worked for me in sweepstakes and other aspects of my life.

In 2004 my life changed. My husband had been out of work for about a year and a half. We had been married for 20 years, everything we owned we got when we first got married and it all was in need of repair or needed to be replaced. Money was tight. I had tried part-time jobs that were getting me nowhere.

I knew I had to stop the negative thinking and find a solution. I started thinking maybe I can *win* the things I need, so I started entering mail-in sweepstakes. I treated it like my part-time job. I spent 2-4 hours every evening looking for sweepstakes for the things I "needed" like a new washer.

At first I had thoughts like, "This isn't going to work, and I'm just wasting needed money on stamps." Then I would say to myself, "I need help, this will be worth it." After the first month I won a $50 gift card for a department store. A few months went by and nothing. The washer was squeaking louder! The truck needed new tires. What was I going to do? I started to worry again but I changed my thinking to, "I need help and this is how I will get it." and "Investing money in stamps will pay off."

On Christmas Eve I was baking cookies and I couldn't get the oven door to close. Frustrated I remember saying to myself, "Great! Something else we need to replace. Where is the money going to come from? I need help and I need it NOW!"

Then an *amazing* thing happened. Not more than two minutes later, the UPS truck showed up at my door with a letter stating I had won a $14,000 shopping spree at Sears and a check for $4100 to pay the taxes! What an awesome prize!!

My positive thinking and persistence paid off!! I told the Universe what I needed instead of complaining and feeling sorry for myself and look what happened! I got every appliance replaced, new tires for the truck, new prescription glasses, everything I "needed" and more. I was even able to help other people which made me feel so good. The Law of Attraction truly works. I'm a believer!

I have continued my positive thinking and have won some unbelievable prizes for myself, family and friends. What a great feeling to surprise someone with a prize they didn't expect.

ΩŒ

TIP: Keep a memory box and/or a spreadsheet of all your wins. I have a memory box that I keep all the affidavits, congratulatory letters, ticket stubs, pictures, etc. in. I also keep a spreadsheet tracking all of our wins. Whenever I feel we are having a "dry" spell, I pull out the box or look at the spreadsheet and I instantly <u>feel</u> happy and lucky.

"Be aware of wonder. Live a balanced life—learn some and think some and draw and paint and sing and dance and play and work every day some."
Robert Fulghum

Energy Balancing: Inside & Out

qi (ch$\bar{e}$)
n. the circulating life energy that in Chinese philosophy is thought to be inherent in all things; in traditional Chinese medicine the balance of negative and positive forms in the body is believed to be essential for good health.

Qi in English is often spelled as **chi** or **ch'i**. The Japanese form is **ki**.

Chi is a fundamental concept of everyday Chinese culture, most often defined as "air" or "breath" (for example, the colloquial Mandarin Chinese term for "weather" is *tiān qi*, or the "breath of heaven") and, by extension, "life force" or "spiritual energy" that is part of everything that exists. References to *chi* or similar philosophical concepts as a type of metaphysical energy that sustains living beings are used in many belief systems, especially in Asia.

The c*hi* is what needs to be in perfect balance within and around us to not only attract winnings but to have a joyous and prosperous life. I feel this is what has helped me get to where I am today, not only with contesting, but in life.

There are many ways to balance our inner and outer lives; meditation, visualization, yoga, *tai chi*, acupuncture, massage, *reiki*, and *feng shui*. This is a very short list of the types of activities and practices you can participate in to balance your life, your body, your family, your home, YOU.

Most of these balancing activities and practices have been around, within different cultures, for thousands of years. Many are becoming "mainstream" as our modern culture begins to incorporate ancient customs into our daily lives.

There are hundreds of books and websites that discuss each of these activities, practices and more in great detail. I will give you a very brief overview on two topics: 1) *chakras*, for balancing the inside and 2) *feng shui*, for balancing the outside. There are further resources to be found at the end of this book, on my website, at your local bookstore and on the Internet.

Inside

What's a *Chakra*?
Chakra is a Sanskrit word meaning wheel, or vortex, and it refers to each of the seven energy centers of which our consciousness, our energy system, is composed.

These *chakras*, or energy centers, function as pumps or valves, regulating the flow of energy through our energy system. The functioning of the *chakras* reflects decisions we make concerning how we choose to respond to conditions in our life. We open and close these valves when we decide what to think, and what to feel, and through which perceptual filter we choose to experience the world around us.

The *chakras* are not physical. They are aspects of consciousness in the same way that the auras are aspects of consciousness. The *chakras* are more dense than the auras, but not as dense as the physical body.

196

They interact with the physical body through two major vehicles, the endocrine system and the nervous system. Each of the seven *chakras* is associated with one of the seven endocrine glands, and also with a group of nerves called a plexus. Thus, each *chakra* can be associated with particular parts of the body and particular functions within the body controlled by that plexus or that endocrine gland associated with that *chakra*.

All of your senses, all of your perceptions, all of your possible states of awareness, everything it is possible for you to experience, can be divided into seven categories. Each category can be associated with a particular *chakra*. Thus, the *chakras* represent not only particular parts of your physical body, but also particular parts of your consciousness.

When you feel tension in your consciousness, you feel it in the *chakra* associated with that part of your consciousness experiencing the stress, and in the parts of the physical body associated with that *chakra*. Where you feel the stress depends upon why you feel the stress. The tension in the *chakra* is detected by the nerves of the plexus associated with that *chakra*, and transmitted to the parts of the body controlled by that plexus. When the tension continues over a period of time, or to a particular level of intensity, the person creates a symptom on the physical level.

The symptom speaks a language that reflects the idea that we each create our reality, and the metaphoric significance of the symptom becomes apparent when the symptom is described from that point of view. Thus, rather than saying, "I can't see," the person would describe it as keeping themselves from seeing something. "I can't walk," means the person has been keeping themselves from walking away from a situation in which they are unhappy. And so on.

The symptom served to communicate to the person through their body what they had been doing to

197

themselves in their consciousness. When the person changes something about their way of being, getting the message communicated by the symptom, the symptom has no further reason for being, and it can be released, according to whatever the person allows themselves to believe is possible.

We believe everything is possible.

We believe that anything can be healed. It's just a question of how to do it. Understanding the *chakras* allows you to understand the relationship between your consciousness and your body, and to thus see your body as a map of your consciousness. It gives you a better understanding of yourself and those around you.

What else is there?

Reprinted with permission by The Brofman Foundation for the Advancement of Healing. www.healer.ch

Another good site to visit is Sacred Centers http://sacredcenters.com/chakras.html. They also have good descriptions of what each *chakra* is and what it relates to.

"What we call luck is the inner man externalized. We make things happen to us."
Robertson Davies

Outside

Feng Shui: The art of studying the environment and how energies interact with a home or premise. *Feng Shui* can hasten fulfillment of a good destiny and give a better quality to life.

THE POWER OF PLACE
Whether we choose to believe it or not, we are greatly affected and influenced, for better or for worse, by our surroundings; particularly the atmosphere and layout of our homes. Not only how we feel, but also how we

interact with others, how productive we are, and our resulting life experiences are directly related to our environment. Have you ever visited someone's home or office for the first time and for some strange reason felt out of sorts, ill at ease or just plain anxious while being there? Or had the opposite reaction, felt so wonderful you didn't want to leave? We have all instinctively shared these experiences at one time or another. What we are sensing is the energy or Feng Shui of that place.

Developed over 3,000 years ago in the East, Feng Shui is widely practiced as the science and art of spatial design and object placement which balances and enhances the energy of one's surroundings. This ancient discipline seeks to create harmonious living and working environments to help one achieve optimal health of body, mind and soul. Feng Shui, (pronounced fung shway) are the Chinese words for wind and water, the two greatest forces of nature. It represents the universal energy which flows between heaven and earth, running through and connecting all things.

The Chi in your body acts very similarly to the way the energy in a magnet works; it draws to it and attracts the same type of energy it magnetizes out. If your Chi is sending out energy signals that resonate to a sense of harmony, balance and well being, then it will draw in the things, events and opportunities that will reflect that feeling. It is so important to realize and remember that all the things that you surround yourself with on a daily basis affect the way Chi flows throughout your home. If positive energy is allowed to flow freely through your environment, then the people who live and work there prosper and benefit.

It is a well known fact that everything in the world has its origins in the world of energy. Quantum physics now confirms that everything in our universe is made up of a mass of constantly moving energy. All physical matter, no matter how solid it feels, is in fact, only energy vibrating. Thus everything on this planet is interconnected by the vibrations of life-force energy which flows between them. Even in the empty spaces that we cannot see, energy exists as well. This means that our home, too, is composed of energy; it is not separate from us, but is a direct reflection of who we are, reflecting our inner energy and intentions throughout our lives. The vibrations found in your home can either be life-suppressing or life-enhancing and the primary focus of a Feng Shui practitioner is to assist the home owner in creating an environment that supports and nurtures them in all areas of their life, both mentally and physically. Enhancing and harmonizing the Chi of our environment strengthens and enhances our own personal Chi. This in turn produces the three most sought after attributes of a good life: health, wealth and happiness. It is not a magic bullet or a quick fix; it is simply a method, an important tool that can help us address and deal with all of life's issues. It simply suggests that it is much easier to "go with the flow" rather than to constantly struggle upstream against it.

Just as there are several different schools of martial arts, so to, in the world of Feng Shui. Black Sect Feng Shui is the most recent school of Feng Shui to be introduced to the West and derives in part from Tibetan Buddhism, as taught be Professor Thomas Lin Yun of Berkeley, California. This school of Feng Shui works purposefully and directly with subtle energy systems within your environment in order to create balance and dynamic life change. This approach is multi-disciplined, incorporating psychology, ecology, interior design, color therapy, yin/yang theory, five element theory, common sense and intuition. By using a more holistic approach in all areas of one's life, Black Sect Feng Shui is a truly unique and powerful art in assisting an individual to make positive life changes. An integral part of improving the Feng Shui of a location is the use of the Bagua. For centuries, the Chinese have placed this mystical energy grid on plots of land, houses and rooms to determine the energy characteristics of an environment. The Bagua is basically a map of the eight major life areas that a person can choose to enhance and strengthen—career, knowledge, family, wealth, fame, love and marriage, children and creativity, and helpful people and support.

To locate these areas the Bagua is superimposed like a template or grid over the floor plan of a home, and even on some specific rooms such as a home office and master bedroom, to indicate the drawbacks and benefits of the location and effects on one's life. During a consultation, the practitioner will be suggesting several different remedies and solutions to a client to attract and enhance a positive flow of Chi throughout the home.

NOTE: Got to www.wsfs.com/support/bagua.pdf for a printable Bagua map.

Have you ever wondered if you can use Feng Shui principles to increase your luck to help you win sweepstakes? Well, the answer is definitely YES! By implementing just a few easy cures, you can start to energize your space, free up blocked energy and allow the flow of positive energy bringing more luck into your home and life.

Here are just a few easy solutions that you can start to use today.

Clear out the clutter: All the Feng Shui cures and adjustments in the world cannot override the negative effects of clutter. This is the first and most important step to take when trying to improve the energy of your home or workspace. Clutter can be defined as things which are untidy or disorganized, too many things in too small a space, and anything left unfinished. The more of it you have, the more stagnant energy it attracts

201

to itself. This can be one of the biggest and most serious drains of energy in one's life. Consider the stress you feel by facing a cluttered and disorganized desktop. When you clear your workspace, you also clear your head and become better organized and less stressed. This allows for new possibilities, ideas and creative solutions to enter.

Seek ease and comfort: Design your desk, or sweeping area, so everything you need is easily accessible by turning around in your chair or by reaching across the desktop. And don't forget that comfortable chair with a high back for greater support physically and energetically! Since most of us spend hours in front of a monitor, it's so important to be as comfortable as possible to avoid strain and back ache. This will greatly improve your own personal Chi level.

Don't skimp on lighting: Make sure you have adequate lighting and position your light source so it does not create any harsh shadows on your desk. Right-handed people should direct the light over their left shoulder and lefties over their right shoulder for optimum efficiency. If space permits, and it fits in with your decor scheme, treat yourself to a beautiful desk top lamp. Whenever possible try to use full spectrum lighting which imitates the full spectrum of natural sunlight. This newer form of lighting is becoming more main stream as people are looking for more ways to boost their energy and improve their health.

Beautify your surroundings: It's so important to surround yourself with art and accessories that make you feel uplifted and happy. Good Feng Shui means positioning yourself amongst furniture you find beautiful and functional. Stop and think for a moment about the symbolic meaning of the art and accessories you choose to surround yourself with. Remember, everything gives off its own form of energy and is speaking to you daily on a subconscious level. You will either be drained or energized by your surroundings and possessions.

Sit in the power position: Never sit at your desk with your back to the door as this will drain your energy and can make you feel like being stuck in a powerless position. If this situation can't be avoided, place or hang a small mirror in front of you to reflect the door so you can always see someone entering the room. Being startled from behind creates stress and insecurity. If possible, try to have a solid wall behind your chair as this represents more support in your life. If it's impossible to sit in this position, at least use a high back chair.

Water fountains: Try placing a soothing table top water fountain either on your desk or in the room you work in. Water is the giver of life and also represents and attracts the flow of opportunities and abundance into our life. Not only are fountains beautiful to look at but as an added health benefit the movement of water releases negative ions into the environment constantly cleaning the air we breathe. They have become a popular decorating accessory in their own right. Why not try one and feel the difference. Always remember to keep the water clean and topped up. And, don't forget to clean the pump of air born dust on a regular basis and you'll receive years of enjoyment from this cure.

Plant life: Another great and easy to install cure is plants. Be creative, if space allows, by placing a large beautiful plant or a group of plants in an empty corner. Life attracts positive energy into a space. And don't forget to add a touch of color to your desk by adding a blooming plant or a vase of fresh cut flowers. To attract more wealth, try using a Chinese "money tree" or a vase with eight stalks of bamboo. Eight is the number that represents wealth and prosperity.

Color: Last but not least, and one of the most overlooked cures is the use of color. All colors from soft pastel shades or rich vibrant bold colors can be included in your decor in small or large amounts. The colors we surround ourselves on a daily basis have a great affect on how we feel. Try experimenting with the color of your walls and go with your instinct, using ones that are your favorite. Try bringing in small splashes of color in your accessories. Look at the color of the artwork on your walls. Maybe it's time for a change? Remember; only buy art that you absolutely love. This will work best on enhancing your own personal energy. It's important to realize that it's not how much you spend on the accessory or how large it is. It's the "intention" you place behind it when you purchase it and again when you install it. Remember, where intention goes, energy flows!

Wherever in your home or workplace you choose to use Feng Shui, you can positively enhance your health, wealth, happiness, and luck. How you enhance and nurture your physical environment will determine how your environment will support and sustain your body, mind, and spirit. *May the good Chi be with you.*

Katherine and Russ Loader, owners of Power of Place, are experts at translating the complex principles of Feng Shui into a language which we can all understand and readily apply to our homes and businesses. (905) 725-7999 www.powerofplace.com

"The universe operates through dynamic exchange…giving and receiving are different aspects of the flow of energy in the universe. And in our willingness to give that which we seek, we keep the abundance of the universe circulating in our lives."
Deepak Chopra

You Get What You Give

It is my personal observation that the people that post the most contests, help others with answers and in general, share, seem to post the most wins. This principle goes back thousands of years. (See chapter, *Join a Sweeping Club*.)

Deepak Chopra wrote a book, *The Seven Spiritual Laws of Success*. I feel that law number two, the Law of Giving, helps describe my theory; *the more I share, the more I win*. Statistically, the opposite should be true. The more people that enter a sweepstakes should decrease my odds of winning. However, I believe the opposite to be true, "I can't lose helping others win".

I share/post as many sweepstakes, answers, and help as often as I can to as many groups as I can. I know there are people within those groups entering many more sweepstakes than I do. Yet, in 2004, 2005, 2006 *and* 2007 I won 100+ sweepstakes. Why do I win 5, 10, 15+ sweepstakes every month (month after month)? Why have I not paid for a trip in four years? I believe it directly ties into the Law of Giving.

> That is why you must give and receive in order to keep wealth and affluence—or anything you want in life—circulating in your life.

> The word affluence comes from the root word "*affluere*," which means "to flow to." The word affluence means "to flow in abundance." Money is really a symbol of the life energy we exchange and the life energy we use as a result of the service we provide to the universe. Another word for money is "currency," which also reflects the flowing nature of energy. The word currency comes from the Latin word "*currere*" which means "to run" or to flow.

> Therefore, if we stop the circulation of money—if our only intention is to hold on to our money and hoard it—since it is life energy, we will stop its circulation back into our lives as well. In order to keep that energy coming to us, we have to keep the energy circulating. Like a river, money must keep flowing, otherwise it

begins to stagnate, to clog, to suffocate and strangle its very own life force. Circulation keeps it alive and vital.

Every relationship is one of give and take. Giving engenders receiving, and receiving engenders giving. What goes up must come down; what goes out must come back. In reality, receiving is the same thing as giving, because giving and receiving are different aspects of the flow of energy in the universe. And if you stop the flow of either, you interfere with nature's intelligence.

The more you give, the more you will receive, because you will keep the abundance of the universe circulating in your life. In fact, anything that is of value in life only multiplies when it is given. That which doesn't multiply through giving is neither worth giving nor worth receiving. If, through the act of giving, you feel you have lost something, then the gift is not truly given and will not cause increase. If you give grudgingly, there is no energy behind that giving.

It is the intention behind your giving and receiving that is the most important thing. The intention should always be to create happiness for the giver and receiver, because happiness is life-supporting and life-sustaining and therefore generates increase. The return is directly proportional to the giving when it is unconditional and from the heart. That is why the act of giving has to be joyful—the frame of mind has to be one in which you feel joy in the very act of giving. Then the energy behind the giving increases many times over.

Practicing the *Law of Giving* is actually very simple: if you want joy, give joy to others; if you want love, learn to give love; if you want attention and appreciation, learn to give attention and appreciation; if you want material affluence, help others to become materially affluent. In fact, the easiest way to get what you want is to help others get what they want. This principle works equally well for individuals, corporations, societies, and nations. If you want to be blessed with all the good things in life learn to silently bless everyone with all the good things in life.

From the book *The Seven Spiritual Laws of Success* © 1994, Deepak Chopra. Reprinted by permission of Amber-Allen Publishing, Inc. P.O. Box 6657, San Rafael, CA 94903. All rights reserved.

"Every action generates a force of energy that returns to us in like kind...what we sow is what we reap. And when we choose actions that bring happiness and success to others, the fruit of our karma is happiness and success."
Deepak Chopra

Good Karma

Galatians 6:7 Do not be deceived. God will not be made a fool. **For a person will reap what he sows**, 6:8 because the person who sows to his own flesh will reap corruption from the flesh, but the one who sows to the Spirit will reap eternal life from the Spirit.

The bible states you reap what you sow. You sow good fortune for others; you reap good fortune for yourself. This also ties back into the Law of Attraction—like attracting like.

I believe the expression *"cheaters never win."* You may cheat, and you may win that particular sweepstakes, but you will lose somewhere else in your life. It is not worth cheating.

Gary Zukav spoke eloquently in his book Soul Stories about how the cycle of getting what you give ties us with the Universe.

Another gift that you get from the Universe is an experience that is perfect for you. This gift comes each moment from the time you were born until you die.

You and the Universe create this gift together. You decide what it will be, and the Universe gives it to you. That is the Golden Rule—what you do to people, people do to you. It is also called karma. If you don't like what people do to you, you can change that by doing things different to them. That is how you and the Universe work together. Each moment you choose a new gift, and, when the time is right, the Universe gives it to you.

Each day brings gifts that you have ordered, and each day you place more orders. You do this by setting you intentions, and then acting on them. The Universe takes your orders, and delivers them. Everyone gets what she or he ordered. If you order fear, you get it. If you order love, you get it.

When you order, you share with the Universe. When your order is filled, the Universe shares with you. Complaining about your gifts is walking in the fog. Recognizing your gifts—and who ordered them—is walking in the sunshine.

Walking in the sunshine is clarity.

Reprinted with the permission of Simon & Schuster Adult Publishing Group from *SOUL STORIES* by Gary Zukav. Copyright © 2000 by Gary Zukav

"Gratitude is one of the easiest and most powerful ways to transform your life. If you become truly grateful, you will magnetize absolute joy to you everywhere you go, and in everything you do."
Rhonda Byrnes

STORY: It is important to thank the sponsors when you win. Gratitude and karma go hand-in-hand.

ෂාცඃ

Terry—Fairport, NY
It is important to always thank the sponsors when you win. For smaller wins I usually go to the sponsor's website and use their "Contact Us" feature to email a thank you. For larger wins, I send a hand-written thank you note.

ෂාცඃ

"The Universe rewards action."
Jack Canfield

Just do it!

I enter almost every sweepstakes I come across. (I would enter more except I do not have the time.) In sales it is called a numbers game. The more prospects you call on, the more sales you are going to make. Similarly, I believe the more sweepstakes I enter, the more sweepstakes I am going to win.

Making Your Own Luck

Lynne's luck started when she happened to come across a newspaper article describing how a woman had won several impressive competition prizes. Lynne therefore decided to enter a crossword competition and won £10. A few weeks later she entered another competition and won three sports bikes. Shortly afterwards, she went to an interview for a position teaching an evening class in fashion design. There was a coffee jar on the interviewer's desk and it had a competition entry form on it. Lynne was drawn to this and asked if she could have the label. The interviewer asked why she wanted it and Lynne told her about how she had won some competitions. The interviewer asked her to come teach two evening classes—one on fashion design and one on how to win competitions. Lynne accepted the offer and also started to enter lots more competitions. Her winning streak continued and she won lots more prizes, including two cars and several holidays abroad.

Interestingly, these competition wins allowed Lynne to achieve her lifelong ambition of becoming a freelance writer. In 1992 she wrote a book on winning competitions. To publicize the book, a press release was sent to her local paper and they published an article about her work. The next day, the story was picked up by the national newspapers and she was invited to appear on several television shows. As a result, Lynne was invited to write newspaper articles on winning competitions. In 1996 she received a telephone call from a major daily newspaper. They had seen her work and asked her to write a daily competition column for them. Her column, 'Win with Lynne', was highly successful and ran for many years.

Lynne has fulfilled many of her lifelong ambitions, been happily married for over forty years and has a wonderful family life. Like many people involved in my research, Lynne attributes much of her success to good fortune.

Wendy is a 40-year-old housewife. She considers herself lucky in many aspects of her life, but is especially fortunate when it comes to winning competitions. On average, she wins about three prizes a week. Some of these prizes are quite small, but many have been substantial. In the last five years she has won large cash prizes and several major holidays abroad. Wendy certainly seems to have a magical ability to win competitions—and she is not the only one. In the previous chapter I described how Lynne has won several large prizes in competitions, including several cars and holidays.

The same is also true of Joe. Like both Wendy and Lynne, Joe considers himself to be very lucky in many areas of his life. He has been happily married for forty years and has a loving family. However, Joe is especially lucky in competitions, and his recent successes include winning televisions, a day spent on the set of a well-known television soap opera, and several holidays.

What is behind Lynne, Wendy and Joe's winning ways? Their secret is surprisingly simple. They all enter a very large number of competitions.

Each week, Wendy enters about sixty postal competitions, and about seventy Internet-based competitions. Likewise, both Lynne and Joe enter about fifty competitions a week, and their chances of winning are increased with each and every entry. All three of them were well aware that their lucky winning ways are, in reality, due to the large number of competitions they enter. As Wendy explained, 'I am a lucky person, but luck is what you make it. I win a lot of competitions and prizes, but I do put a huge amount of effort into it.'

Joe commented: People always said to me they think I'm very lucky because of the amount of competitions that I win. But then they tell me that they don't enter many themselves, and I think, "Well, if you don't enter, you have no chance of winning." They look at me as being very lucky, but I think you make your own luck ... as I say to them 'You've got to be in to win.'

From the book THE LUCK FACTOR by Dr. Richard Wiseman. Copyright © 2003 Dr. Richard Wiseman. Reprinted by permission of Miramax Books/Hyperion. All rights reserved.

"You inner world, the mental, the emotional and the spiritual, creates your outer world, the physical."
T. Harv Eker

YOU CAN'T WIN IF YOU DON'T ENTER

"Winning is important to me, but what brings me real joy is the experience of being fully engaged in whatever I'm doing."
Phil Jackson

CONCLUSION

If you were new to sweeping when you began reading this book I hope I have turned you into a savvy sweeper. If you were a seasoned sweeper, I hope I have helped you learn a few tips, tricks and about the new technologies. My goal when I began writing this book was to teach people about the hobby of sweeping and hopefully, have as much fun as I do dreaming, entering and winning.

STORY: Lynn was a very wonderful woman who was as passionate about sweeping as I am. Sadly, Lynn passed away in 2005 and I never had the opportunity to meet her in person. I wanted to share with you her luckiest day. May we all be as lucky as Lynn one day.

୧୦୧ଓ

One of the most exciting days of my life was the day I started getting dressed to go and pick-up the car I had won. My husband called and while we were talking the "call waiting beep" warned me another call was on the line. It was a judging agency asking me to answer a skill testing question. I answered correctly so they informed me I won a trip to Greece. Ken was still on hold so I excitedly told him about my latest win. As we were talking the mail man arrived with a registered letter informing me I had won a trip to Mexico! You can imagine Ken's surprise when I told him I just won a second trip to Mexico. A car and two trips all in one day! I'm still working on topping that one.

Extract from *WINNING WAYS* by Lynn Banks Goutbeck and Melanie Rockett. Used by permission of Proof Positive Productions Ltd. www.proofpositive.com

৪৩৪৩

Remember, *you can't win if you don't enter.*
GOOD LUCK & HAVE FUN!

RECOMMENDED READING

Contest Guru's Guide to Winning Sweepstakes
by Melanie Rockett

Your guide to an exciting and lucrative hobby.
Find out:

- What makes sweepstakes different from a raffle, from a lottery.
- Where to find sweepstakes.
- Links to the best offline and online newsletters.
- What laws govern contests, sweeps, etc. (the U.S. and Canada).
- What an HDF is and how to create one.
- How to draw UPC codes.
- How to get organized for off line contesting.
- Tools for online contesting.
- Links to the best sweeps sites.
- Where to find contests.
- The FOUR winning ways Secrets.
- Meet some BIG winners.
- Do contest winners pay taxes?
- Contesting tools and resources.
- How the principles of attraction can help you create LUCK.
  ...and more!

Download your FREE COPY of Contest Guru while it is still free. Visit www.contestguru.com, sign up for the newsletter and the book is yours!

Excuse Me, Your *Life* is Waiting
by Lynn Grabhorn

*never before told, because it
was never before known*

In an upbeat, humorous, and somewhat irreverent style, Lynn Grabhorn introduces us to the amazing Law of Attraction, a new and rapidly unfolding realm of feelings that physicians, scientists, physicists, and theologians are coming to believe is very, very real.

Excuse Me, Your LIFE Is Waiting clarifies why most of our dreams have never materialized, why the majority of us have lived with all-too-empty bank accounts, tough relationships, failing health, and often spiritually unfulfilling lives. Most importantly, in an easy-to-read style peppered with logical explanations, simple steps, and true-life examples, Lynn Grabhorn shows us how to turn it all around—right now.

The most unconscious thing we do all day long is what actually creates and molds every moment of every day of our lives. And what is this "thing" that governs us so forcefully? Feelings! Grabhorn reveals how our feelings make our lives what they are—not positive thinking, or sweat and strain, or good or bad luck, or even smarts, but feelings: good ones, bad ones, up ones, down ones, and all the ones in between.

Until now, we have run our lives on a default setting, manifesting experiences by happenstance rather than intent. Now, with no effort other than paying attention to how we're feeling, the play becomes our deliberate creation, and the world becomes our oyster.

How to Win Lotteries Sweepstakes and Contests in the 21st Century (2nd Edition)
by Steve Ledoux

Learn the Winning Secrets of America's Sweepstakes King!
In this completely revised and updated second edition of his best-selling book (over 75,000 copies sold!), Steve Ledoux reveals the secrets that have enabled him to win thousands and thousands of dollars in cash and prizes. He also shares his skills in choosing lottery

numbers, entering and winning sweepstakes and contests, and spotting illegal scams in this savvy collection of prize-winning strategies.

Lottery and sweepstakes hopefuls learn how to find the right contests to enter, how to protect themselves from cheaters, and what to expect after winning, including how to deal with the IRS and give interviews to the media. Internet sweepstakes, contests, game shows, and resources complete this guide to winning the jackpot!

Steve Ledoux has won more than 500 sweepstakes and contests and has collected thousands and thousands of dollars in winnings. He has been a winning contestant on Wheel of Fortune, has won all-expenses-paid trips for two to the Caribbean, Hawaii, Jamaica, and Las Vegas, and has won a year's supply of Ben & Jerry's ice cream.

Law of Attraction
by Michael Losier

You're Already Experiencing the Law of Attraction

You may not be aware of it, but a very powerful force is at work in your life. It's called the Law of Attraction and right now it's attracting people, jobs, situations, and relationships to your life—not all of them good! If your life feels as if it's turned south and taken on the characteristics of a bad soap opera, it's time to pick up this book.

This complete how-to reference will teach you how to make the Law of Attraction work for you by helping you eliminate the unwanted from your life and filling it up with the things that give you energy, prosperity, and joy.

You can use the Law of Attraction to make a few changes in your life or do a complete overhaul. You'll find all the directions right here. Discover how easy it is to use the Law of Attraction to:

- Stop attracting things you don't want.
- Increase wealth.
- Find your perfect mate.
- Increase your customer base.
- Clarify your goals and strategies.
- Locate your ideal job.

The Luck Factor
by Richard Wiseman

The revolutionary book that reveals the four scientific principles of luck—and how you can use them to change your life

For over ten years, psychologist Professor Richard Wiseman has been conducting a unique research project, examining the behaviour of over a thousand volunteers who considered themselves "lucky" or "unlucky". The results reveal a radical new way of looking at luck:

- You hold the key to creating your luck.
- There are four simple behavioural techniques that are scientifically proven to help you attract good fortune.
- You can use these principles to revolutionize every area of your life—including your relationships, personal finances and career.

For the first time, the elusive luck factor has been identified. Using the simple techniques described in this book, you can learn how to increase your levels of luck, confidence and success.

The Power of Positive Thinking
by Norman Vincent Peale

> *"This book is written with the sole objective of helping the reader achieve a happy, satisfying, and worthwhile life."*
> Dr. Norman Vincent Peale

This classic book will help you to learn how to:
- Break the worry habit.
- Get other people to like you.
- "Energize your life"—to give yourself the vitality and initiative needed to carry out your ambitions and hopes.
- Avoid "the jitters" in your daily work.
- Believe in yourself and in everything you do.
- Live a controlled, relaxed life no matter how fast the pace may be.
- Build a new power and determination through a simple formula that really works.

218

- Develop the power to reach your goals.
- Think the kind of thoughts that lead you to a fuller life and satisfying success.

Faith in Yourself Makes Good Things Happen to You

The Prize Winner of Defiance, Ohio
by Terry Ryan

The Prize Winner of Defiance, Ohio introduces Evelyn Ryan, an enterprising woman who kept poverty at bay with wit, poetry and perfect prose during the "contest era" of the 1950s and 1960s. Evelyn's winning ways defied the church, her alcoholic husband, and antiquated views of housewives. To her, flouting convention was a small price to pay when it came to raising her six sons and four daughters.

Graced with a rare appreciation for life's inherent hilarity, Evelyn turned every financial challenge into an opportunity for fun and profit. The story of the irrepressible woman, whose clever entries are worthy of Erma Bombeck, Dorothy Parker, and Ogden Nash, is told by her daughter Terry with an infectious joy that shows how a winning spirit will always triumph over poverty.

Soul Stories
by Gary Zukav

Writing with profound psychological and spiritual insight, prizewinning author Gary Zukav has had a major impact on the consciousness of millions. In his *New York Times* number-one best seller, *The Seat of the Soul*, he explained how the expansion of human perception beyond the five senses leads to a new understanding of power—the alignment of the personality with the soul—which in turn leads to an awareness of our extraordinary creative abilities. Now, in one of the most important and useful books you will ever read, Soul Stories, Zukav shows how this new understanding of power—authentic power—transforms lives in countless ways.

Soul Stories is filled with marvelous stories that show how concepts such as intuition, harmony, cooperation, sharing, and reverence for life actually express themselves in people's lives. Best of all, the stories lead to practical advice on how you can discover your own Soul Stories

219

and the truths they reveal about the deepest sources of your being. Wonderfully readable, *Soul Stories* is a wise and inspirational book.

The Seven Spiritual Laws of Success
by Deepak Chopra

This is a book you will cherish for a lifetime, for within its pages are the secrets to making all your dreams come true. In *The Seven Spiritual Laws of Success*, Deepak Chopra distills the essence of his teachings into seven simple, yet powerful principles that can easily be applied to create success in all areas of your life.

Based on natural laws which govern all of creation, this book shatters the myth that success is the result of hard work, exacting plans, or driving ambition.

In *The Seven Spiritual Laws of Success,* Deepak Chopra offers a life-altering perspective on the attainment of success: Once we understand our true nature and learn to live in harmony with natural law, a sense of well-being, good health, fulfilling relationships, energy and enthusiasm for life, and material abundance will spring forth easily and effortlessly.

Filled with timeless wisdom and practical steps you can apply right away, this is a book you will want to read and refer to again and again.

Surreal Gourmet Bites: show-stoppers and conversation starters
by Bob Blumer

With Surreal Gourmet Bites, Bob Blumer elevates party food into wow-inspiring, how-did-you-think-of-that creations.

It's no wonder Bob's called The Surreal Gourmet. He's an artist when it comes to food. And these little masterpieces are as lighthearted as the party itself: Chinese Snow Cones (chicken salad with ginger vinaigrette in baked wonton cones); Coconut Shrimp Lollypops (coconut-crusted shrimp with an apricot-ginger dipping sauce); S'mores Shooters (amaretto hot chocolate with roasted marshmallows). Each recipe comes complete with ways to simplify the dish, level of skill needed, prep times, and even suggestions for music to cook by and beverage pairings. Pick one or two to set the stage for an impressive dinner or several for a fabulous cocktail party that will keep your guests talking about the food all the way home.

The beauty of Blumer's recipes is that they are foolproof—even for most culinary challenged cooks. They rely on ingredients found at the local grocery store that are brought to life with heavy-handed infusion of fresh herbs and spices. These whimsically presented bites are simple enough for impromptu gatherings, yet memorable enough to become addictive. With Surreal Gourmet Bites, the food will be the life of the party.

Bob Blumer is the creator and host of the Food Network Canada show The Surreal Gourmet. He lives in the Hollywood Hills where his other car is a Toastermobile. This is his fourth book.

Winning Sweepstakes: The Proven Strategy
by Jeffrey & Robin Sklar

Not all sweepstakes are created equal…Some are much easier to win than others. Learn how to recognize and win the best, most "winnable" ones!

Jeffrey and Robin Sklar, publishers of Winning Sweepstakes Newsletter, are nationally recognized authorities at winning sweepstakes. They wrote Winning Sweepstakes: The Proven Strategy to share the proven winning strategies they have developed since winning the first sweepstake they entered in 1981. Since then, the couple has won tens of thousands of dollars in sweepstakes prizes…not by sheer luck but rather by devoting their entries to the best sweepstakes with the best prizes and best odds of winning.

They are acknowledged as the first players to apply computing science to sweepstake playing and are sometimes referred to as "Mr. And Mrs. Sweepstakes" and the "Odds Couple." The Sklars and their sweepstakes successes have been featured on the Today Show, Nightline, the Wall Street Journal Report and in Money Magazine.

This book stands alone as the only comprehensive authoritative "how-to" source of information evaluating, entering and winning sweepstakes. Here are just a few of the hundreds of tips you'll learn:

221

- 13 ways to spot the easiest-to-win sweepstakes
- Which sweepstakes have terrible odds and are a waste of your time
- How to win unclaimed prizes in second chance sweepstakes
- Which industries consistently sponsor the best sweepstakes
- Exactly how many entries you need to win game sweepstakes
- How NOT to be among the up to 40% disqualified entries
- How to interpret the official rules
- 8 ways to make your contest entries more original
- How to maximize the edge against you in state lotteries
- Plus much, much more!

REMEMBER! To win regularly, it is not enough to enter often, you must ENTER SMART! Winning Sweepstakes: The Proven Strategy reveals how sweepstakes and contests work, and how to make the odds win for you!

11482974R0013

Made in the USA
Lexington, KY
07 October 2011